A Naturalist's Blue Ridge Parkway

A Naturalist's Blue Ridge Parkway

by David T. Catlin

The University of Tennessee Press

Knoxville

Cloth: 1st printing, 1984.
Paper: 1st printing, 1984; 2nd printing, 1992.

The paper in this book meets the minimum requirements of the American
National Standard for Permanence of Paper for Printed Library Materials.
∞ The binding materials have been chosen for strength and durability.

Library of Congress Cataloging in Publication Data

Catlin, David T.
  A naturalist's Blue Ridge Parkway.

  Bibliography: p.
  1. Natural history—Blue Ridge Parkway (Va. and N.C.)
2. Natural history—Appalachian Mountains. I. Title
QH104.5B5C38   1984   508.755   83-26003
ISBN 0–87049–426–0 (cloth: alk. paper)
ISBN 0–87049–430–9 (pbk.: alk. paper)

Color photographs by David Catlin. Black and white photographs by David
Catlin, with additional photographs by Tom R. Johnson on pages 112, 119, 122,
159; by Jay Shuler on page 127; by Bill Duyck on pages 130, 131, 132; by U.S.
Forest Service on pages 72, 171; by National Park Service on pages 26, 70, 85,
165, 166, 168; by Missouri Department of Conservation on pages 134, 136, 137,
152, 156. Sketches by Tom R. Johnson.

Map 1, reprinted from Harley E. Jolley, *The Blue Ridge Parkway* (Knoxville:
Univ. of Tennessee Press, 1969); Map 2, by John D. Lindner.

For my parents,
who helped make it possible,
and for Jane,
who helped make it real

Contents

Contents

Illustrations

Maps

Acknowledgments

This book covers a broad range of subjects, and as a result I have had to draw on the expertise of many individuals, organizations, and agencies in my preparation of it. I would like to thank everyone who helped me. Though there are too many people to allow me to name everyone, I would like to acknowledge that this book would not have been possible without their assistance.

Some individuals made especially significant contributions. My advisors during my stay at the University of Washington – Dr. Grant Sharpe, Dr. Linda Brubaker, and Dr. David Manuwal – all reviewed my completed manuscript and provided large doses of help and encouragement. Dr. R. Wayne Van Devender of Appalachian State University, Jerry Bartholomew of the Montana Bureau of Mines and Geology, Randall Kendrick of the National Park Service, and my good friend Jay Shuler also read early drafts and made many helpful suggestions for improvement. Tom R. Johnson of the Missouri Department of Conservation, Professor J. Dan Pittillo of Western Carolina University, and W.H. Martin generously reviewed individual chapters.

In addition, many people provided me with information and materials based on their own experience along the Blue Ridge Parkway and in the southern Appalachians generally. They include Robert James Brown, Costello Craig, Bill Duyck, Tom Haggerty, David S. Lee, Joe Mickey, Jr., Dr. Orson K. Miller, Myriam Moore, Robyn Nolen, William Palmer, Gary Swihart, Dr. Marcus B. Simpson, Jr., Dr. Garrett Smathers, Michael Tove, Roger Stone, and John Roth. I'd also like to express my appreciation to the many agencies and schools these people represent.

Special thanks are due O.V. Olsen, Ken Ball, Neil de Jong, Andy Kardos, Hoyt Rath, Gene Parker, Tom Olsen, Butch Kelly, Gussie Carrell, Tom Booker, and the dozens of other Blue Ridge Parkway people who helped in a variety of ways. Similarly, I'd like to thank the editors and staff of the University of Tennessee Press for their expertise and patience.

Finally, a very special thank you to Jane Barlow for her editing, her typing, and her unflagging moral support.

Map 1. The Blue Ridge Parkway

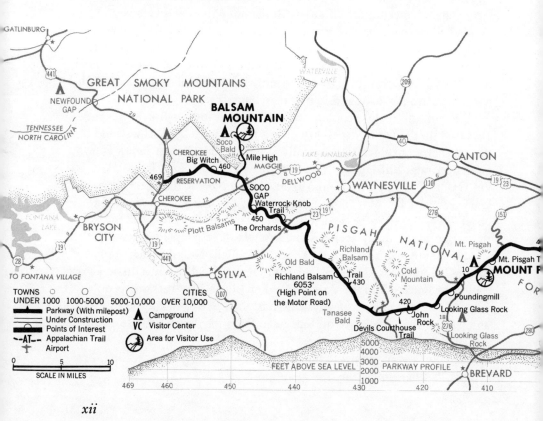

GATLINBURG

441

GREAT SMOKY MOUNTAINS
NATIONAL PARK

NEWFOUND
GAP

TENNESSEE
NORTH CAROLINA

29

CHEROKEE
Big Witch

460

469

RESERVATION

CHEROKEE

2

12

Plott Balsams

12

Old Bald

FONTANA
LAKE

9

19

28

BRYSON
CITY

441

19

107

SYLVA

TO FONTANA VILLAGE

TOWNS
UNDER 1000   1000-5000   5000-10,000   OVER 10,000

Parkway (With milepost)
Under Construction
Points of Interest
AT Appalachian Trail
Airport

0   5   10
SCALE IN MILES

**BALSAM
MOUNTAIN**

Soco
Bald

Mile High
MAGGIE

8

DELLWOOD

SOCO
GAP

Waterrock Knob
Trail

450

The Orchards

Richland Balsam
6053'
(High Point on
the Motor Road)

Richland
Balsam

Trail
430

CITIES

Campground
VC Visitor Center
Area for Visitor Use

WATERVILLE
LAKE

209

LAKE JUNALUSKA

40

19

WAYNESVILLE

23

110

7

PISGAH

18

Cold
Mountain

Tanasee
Bald

Devils Courthouse
Trail

420

John
Rock

5000
4000
3000
2000
1000

FEET ABOVE SEA LEVEL

PARKWAY PROFILE

469   460   450   440   430   420   410

CANTON

19

23

276

151

Mt. Pisgah

10

Mt. Pisgah T
MOUNT P

Poundingmill

Looking Glass Rock

18

276

Looking Glass
Rock

NATIONAL

FOR

280

BREVARD

16

xii

Introduction

Begin at Rockfish Gap, the north end of the Blue Ridge Parkway, and drive all the way to its southern terminus at the Oconaluftee River; you will travel a distance longer than that from Washington, D.C., to Boston yet never pass a fast-food restaurant or drive-in movie theater. There is nowhere else in the eastern United States where a person can travel so far completely surrounded by trees.

The Blue Ridge Parkway is a 469-mile scenic road that connects Shenandoah National Park in Virginia with Great Smoky Mountains National Park in North Carolina and Tennessee. The road between winds across ridges and summits and through gaps and hollows of the southern Appalachian Mountains. Other woodland areas in North America, per-

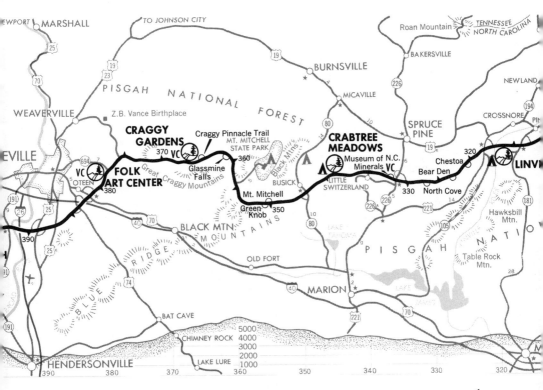

haps, equal this one in grandeur and wildness; none rivals it in ecological complexity. More than one naturalist has found a lifetime of study in the interrelationships of towering tuliptrees, spring-fed streams, black bears, and the ancient rocks that are the southern Appalachians.

It is the mountains that have made this land special. Because these peaks have existed for millions of years, evolution has produced more salamander species here, for instance, than in any other region on earth. Because they thrust their plant and animal residents high into increasingly colder and wetter air, natural communities exist on Appalachian summits that cannot otherwise be found south of upstate New York. In contrast, the neighboring valleys are typically southeastern.

The Blue Ridge Parkway is the gateway to this natural history wonderland. Camp for a night at Otter Creek (Milepost 60.8). You can wake early to the melodious song of the wood thrush, then travel a mere 15 miles south to the heights of Apple Orchard Mountain (Milepost 76.5) and there listen to the thrush's northern cousin (and ecological replace-

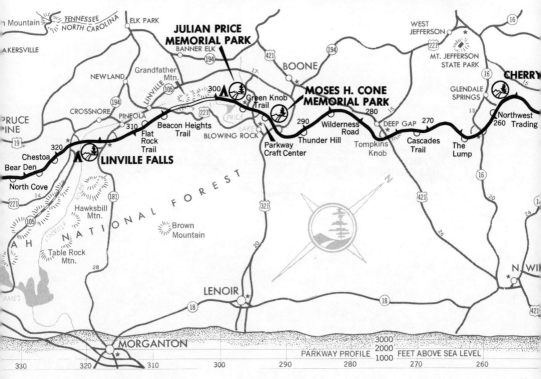

ment), the veery, before the sun has taken the chill from the morning air. Or pause for a moment on the bank of the French Broad River (Milepost 393.5). Here you can stand among river birch and sycamore typical of southeastern stream bottoms, yet after only an hour's drive south find yourself surrounded by a spruce-fir forest similar in many ways to those in northern Maine. The sheltered valleys and windy summits, rocky ridges and rich coves of these mountains are responsible for the diversity here; and the Parkway, in its long, meandering course, fully samples that diversity.

No one book can capture the entire story of this region's natural history; such a task would require a set of encyclopedias hefty enough to fill the trunk of a car. One book should be able, however, to capture the *essence* of that story. It should be able to show visitors why, from a naturalist's perspective, there *is* a Blue Ridge Parkway. I hope that this volume will in some measure achieve that aim.

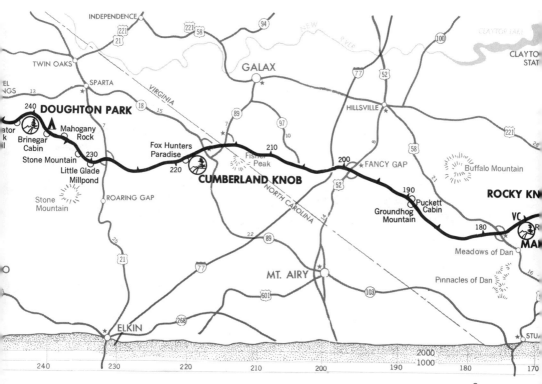

For convenience' sake I have divided the elements of the Parkway's natural history into categories: geology, nonflowering plants, wildflowers, trees, invertebrates, fish, amphibians, reptiles, birds, mammals, and the effects of man are all covered separately. It should be remembered, however, that in nature they are not separated: every stone, every mushroom, every beetle, every raccoon, and every oak is connected to the rest of the natural community in a hundred ways. I have tried to illustrate as many of these connections as possible.

Throughout the book I have attempted to eliminate technical talk and complicated explanations in favor of simpler language. For those interested in more detail, the Appendix contains checklists of the flora and fauna found in many of the recreation areas located along the Parkway, and I have also included a Suggested Reading list.

Finally, I have tried to associate the things mentioned in the text with specific locations where those things can be seen. The Blue Ridge Parkway is provided with mileposts (M.P.) numbered north to south from

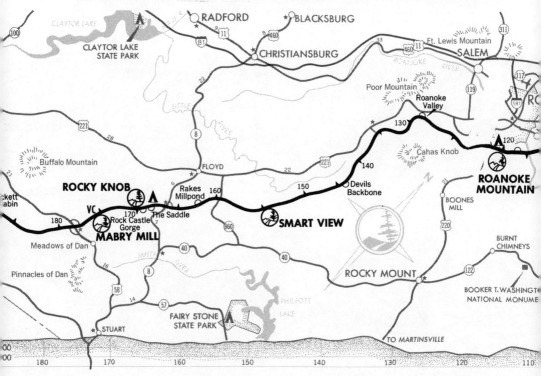

o to 469. References to these are made wherever possible (often with tenths of miles for even more precision).

I hope readers can put these references to practical use. Two-dimensional pages can never have the impact of three-dimensional forests and fields. They cannot convey the land's richness, and they cannot move the soul in the same way. Therefore, I hope you have the opportunity to be not just an "armchair" naturalist, but a "bucket seat" naturalist and a "sore feet" naturalist. Enjoy a visit to the Blue Ridge Parkway, and appreciate the magnificence of its nature in person.

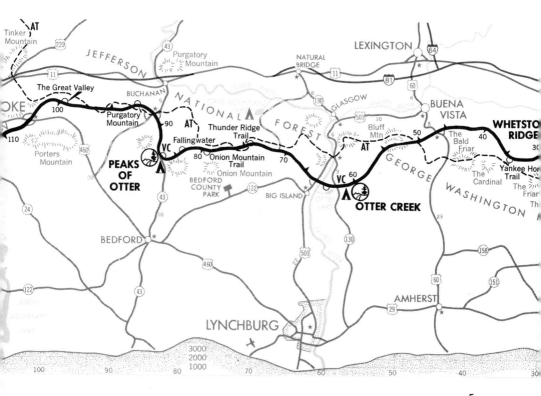

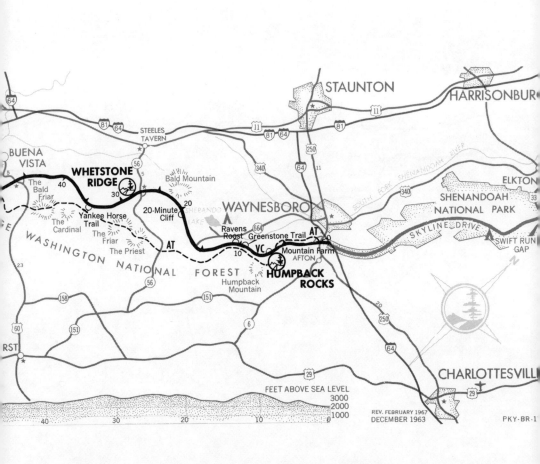

STAUNTON

HARRISONBUR

64

81 64

STEELES
TAVERN

11

81 64

81

BUENA
VISTA

56

WHETSTONE
RIDGE

5

Bald Mountain

340

250

64

11

ELKTON

33

SHENANDOAH
NATIONAL PARK

5

The
Bald
Friar

40

30

WAYNESBORO

SOUTH FORK SHENANDOAH RIVER

340

SKYLINE DRIVE

SWIFT RUN
GAP

20-Minute
Cliff

20

Yankee Horse
Trail

The
Cardinal

The
Friar

The Priest

AT

664

SHERANDO
LAKE

Ravens
Roost

Greenstone Trail

AT

N

23

WASHINGTON NATIONAL FOREST

56

10

VC

Mountain Farm

AFTON

158

Humpback
Mountain

HUMPBACK
ROCKS

60

151

151

6

250

RST

40

30

20

10

64

29

FEET ABOVE SEA LEVEL
3000
2000
1000

REV. FEBRUARY 1967
DECEMBER 1963

CHARLOTTESVILL

29

PKY-BR-1

Geology

More people, it seems to me, are interested in bears and rare yellow ladyslippers than in rocks. Why is this? For one reason, rocks do not appear to move. A bear, on the other hand, may dash across the road through the headlights of your car at any moment. For another reason, rocks do not noticeably change. Much of the excitement in finding a rare ladyslipper comes from knowing that had you stumbled across the plant a week earlier or a week later, it might not have been in bloom. Plants and animals provide our stimulus-hungry minds with action. Rocks appear static.

The visitor who does not take a moment, though, to dabble at least a little in the geology of the Blue Ridge will be missing some fascinating stories and not a few surprises. For rocks do move, and rocks do change. Here in the southern Appalachians, continents have slammed together and earthquakes have shaken the ground. Layers of the earth's crust have crumpled like corrugated cardboard and overlapped in places like shingles on a roof. High plateaus have had great gouges scraped out of them, and even now streams are being "pirated." But because these things occur over spans of millions of years, our senses cannot detect the movement and change. We must take the time to grasp them with our minds.

And the dyed-in-the-wool devotee of the flora and fauna, the visitor who still feels that plants and animals are the main items of interest along the Blue Ridge Parkway, might take note: the geology has affected every living thing here. Without the mountains, there would very likely be no bears or rare yellow ladyslippers in western Virginia and North Carolina. This should be reason enough to understand rocks a little better.

So let us begin this natural history with the geological story.

An Overview of the Southern Appalachians

We are concerned with only a section of the Appalachian mountains. The entire chain extends as a series of ridges and smaller groups of mountains all the way from Newfoundland in maritime Canada, through

Tom R. Johnson

New England and eastern New York, southward into northern Georgia and Alabama. It runs from the northeast to the southwest, then, roughly parallel to the Atlantic coast.

Geographers generally consider the mountains south of central Pennsylvania to be the "southern" Appalachians, and in the interest of simplicity I will use their more general term throughout this guide. Geologists, on the other hand, divide the same area into the "central" and "southern" Appalachians, with the separation between the two occurring at the Roanoke River in Virginia (M.P. 114.8). Both geographers and geologists also divide the Appalachian region into units called provinces. Geographers base these units mostly on the nature of their topography, geologists on the ages and types of rock. Again, I will make use of the geographers' divisions (called *physiographic* provinces) in this description. The provinces are arranged northeast to southwest and parallel to one another in a sequence of long, slender strips. The Piedmont is the first Appalachian province you encounter as you drive west from the Atlantic, a broad rolling plateau whose rock strata—though of similar age to those in the mountains—have been worn nearly flat through the ages. Cross the Piedmont, and you come to the Blue Ridge province. Here the mountains begin in earnest. The Blue Ridge Parkway—as well as Shenandoah National Park and the Great Smoky Mountains National Park—lies almost exclusively in this section.

The best way to acquire an understanding of how the Blue Ridge province is arranged would be to fly the length of it in an airplane. Imaginatively, then, let's do that. Our aircraft takes off from Harrisburg, Pennsylvania, and wings southwest. The Blue Ridge physiographic province begins here somewhat tentatively at South Mountain. It continues as a low ridge or series of ridges down into Virginia. As one looks out the window, a view of thousands of acres of forest indicates that Shenandoah National Park is below. These are the Blue Ridge Mountains we see—a high summit now, stretching for miles, with spurs reaching out on each side. Here the Blue Ridge province is no more than 15 miles across. As we fly south, out of the park now and over the northern section of the Blue Ridge Parkway, we discover that for great stretches, in fact, the province is no more than a single 3,000-foot ridge, separating the Piedmont province to the east from the Valley and Ridge province to the west.

The pattern continues, broken only by several water gaps, all the way

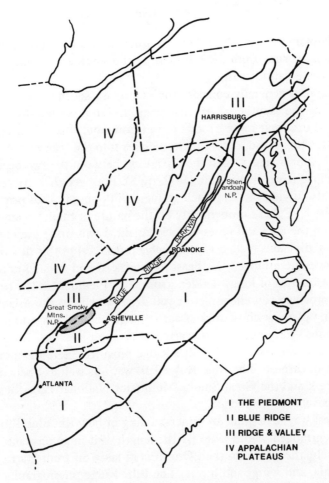

Map 2. The physiographic provinces of the southern Appalachian mountains

to Roanoke, Virginia. We have flown nearly 275 miles over a relatively
constant landscape. As we navigate toward North Carolina, though, the
picture below us changes. South of where the Roanoke River penetrates
the Blue Ridge, the province widens into a broad, rolling plateau. On its
eastern edge the mountains thrust upward from the low hills of the Piedmont province in a steep escarpment. Instead of dropping back down
into valley on the western side, however, it now levels off into a tableland
that widens as we go south. The topography remains hilly, but the many

1. The narrowness of the northern Blue Ridge is especially apparent just north of Roanoke, Virginia. The Parkway in this section twists from one side of the ridge to the other.

fields and pastures visible to us from the air indicate that it is much flatter than the ridgetops of the northern Blue Ridge.

Gradually, the entire province becomes more rugged. The range that forms the eastern rampart of the southern Appalachians continues to retain the geographer's label "Blue Ridge Mountains", but in North Carolina and Tennessee the western edge of the Blue Ridge province – nearly 75 miles away at its widest point – is dominated by ranges with other names. Most notable among these are the Great Smoky Mountains. And piled perpendicularly across the province like crude rungs on a massive ladder are cross ranges: the Black Mountains, the Craggy Mountains, the Cowee Mountains, the Nantahalas, the Balsams, and others. The pilot pulls our plane into a climb; here we must clear dozens of summits over 6,000 feet in elevation. They include Mount Mitchell – at 6,684 feet, the highest peak in eastern North America.

The mountains of the Blue Ridge physiographic province extend south across the borders of Tennessee and North Carolina into Georgia and the corner of South Carolina, but only for a short distance. They end soon enough for us to put down on the runway at Atlanta, after a flight of some 600 miles and a rapid overview of Blue Ridge geography.

For those visitors who either cannot afford to fly or don't want to miss all the details that cannot be experienced from the air, driving the Blue Ridge Parkway is a good alternative. The route is a bit shorter and a little less comprehensive, but otherwise basically the same. Beginning where the Skyline Drive of Shenandoah National Park ends – at Rockfish Gap near Waynesboro, Virginia – the Parkway travels along the ridgetop for 115 miles to the Roanoke River. As the road curves from one side of the crest to the other, you are treated to panoramic vistas first of the Virginia Piedmont and then of the pastoral Shenandoah Valley. Especially scenic are the stretches south of Humpback Rocks (M.P. 5.8), near Buena Vista (M.P. 45.6), and along Thunder Ridge (M.P. 74.7). The bridge over the James River (M.P. 63.7) provides an excellent view of the deep gap that water has carved through the mountains here.

South of Roanoke the Parkway meanders mostly across the rolling farmland of the widening Blue Ridge plateau. Should you begin to forget that you are still in the mountains, however, you need only stop at places like the Smart View Picnic Area (M.P. 154.5) or Fox Hunter's Paradise

Overlook (M.P. 218.6) to view the 2,000-foot drop to the piedmont and remind yourself of your elevation.

By the time auto travelers reach the vicinity of Boone, North Carolina (M.P. 290), they are staring up at summits the airplane passengers looked down on. Just south of Blowing Rock the Parkway skirts the flanks of Grandfather Mountain (M.P. 303), at 5,964 feet, the tallest peak in what geographers call the Blue Ridge Mountains. Then, at M.P. 354, the road turns west, leaving for the first time the eastern part of the Blue Ridge province and putting the Blue Ridge Mountains behind. The visitor is led now into the lofty cross ranges of the western Blue Ridge: first the Blacks, passing very near Mount Mitchell at M.P. 355.3, then the Craggies.

Finally, after dropping down into the lower basin area around Asheville, North Carolina, the Parkway climbs across the last three of the cross ranges it will traverse: the Pisgah Ledge, the Balsams, and the Plott Balsams. As it does so, the road reaches its highest point—6,053 feet—on Richland Balsam (M.P. 431). From where the parkway ends at the border of the Great Smoky Mountains National Park, it is a drive of only 15 miles to the line that marks the North Carolina–Tennessee border and the crest of the Smokies. Travel this distance, and you will reach the western edge of the Blue Ridge province.

How the Mountains Were Formed

The present configuration of the land's surface in the Blue Ridge is easy enough to see and explore. Introductory geology classes from universities neighboring the Parkway frequently tour it on field trips. They learn about which mountains belong to which ranges, about where there are igneous rocks and where there are metamorphic ones, and about which ocean a raindrop will finally reach if it falls on one side of a ridge or the other. These aspects of geology are fairly straightforward.

However, the full geological story of the southern Appalachians includes more than information on what the mountains are like now. Essential to an understanding of the geology of a place is an idea of its geologic history. Why are there mountains here and not in eastern Virginia and North Carolina? How did they come to be gentle and rounded com-

2. Standing alone and nearly 6,000 feet in elevation, Grandfather Mountain dominates vistas for miles in every direction.

pared to Colorado's Rockies or California's Sierra Nevada? What has created gemstones in one place but not in another?

Geologists have suggested answers to all these questions and others as well. Their answers are based on years of work sorting through the often cryptic messages contained in visible geology.

Because the Blue Ridge is an area complex in geological detail, many of their answers are also complicated. Not all of the mountains' stories lend themselves well to simplification. Nonetheless, I will narrate here in a very basic way some of the generally accepted explanations of the origins of the southern Appalachians. Readers interested in more information should investigate works listed as Suggested Reading.

It is generally agreed now that the crust of the earth is made up of huge, rigid plates of rock that float on the hot, more plastic material of the mantle beneath. Picture the vast sheets of ice that cover the Arctic Ocean, and you will have an analogous view of how geologists envision the surface of our planet. Furthermore, like Arctic ice floes, the plates of the earth's crust are always moving—grinding together, fusing, and breaking apart again as time passes.

Of course, the movement is far too slow for us to notice. As centuries go by, however, the slow creep of these plates has significant effects. Where two of them are moving away from each other, molten rock from deep within the mantle fills the gap. (This is occurring today, for example, along a mountainous ridge down the center of the Atlantic Ocean, as two plates slide apart at a rate of an inch or so a year.)

More important to our discussion is what happens in the zone where two plates collide. When the leading edges of both sections consist of oceanic crust, a deep trough forms as one crustal block is wedged beneath the other. There are, however, land masses lodged in these plates as logs might be frozen in our ice floes. Some are only island chains; others are entire continents. When these great land masses collide, they grind slowly together over millions of years, and all sorts of geological events occur. Slabs of the crust pile up in folds like throw rugs sliding together on a slick floor. Great sections of crustal material thousands of feet thick slide one atop another as if they were cards in a shuffled deck. Magma and steam rise up through cracks and fissures far below ground, and their heat remelts and changes the subsurface rocks. Earthquakes rumble as stress is released. Eventually, the two plates may fuse into one, only to split again epochs later along some new seam.

Typical of the oldest rocks found in the southern Appalachians is a type called "Cranberry Gneiss" (pronounced "nice"), found in north-western North Carolina. (It can easily be seen along the trail to Linville Falls, M.P. 316.4.) At the time of its formation more than one billion years ago, the area that later became the Blue Ridge was undergoing a long period of metamorphism; that is, the rock that existed then was be-ing heated and reformed into new rock types at great depths. In some places, masses of molten material from deep within the earth were in-jected into these crustal layers.

Millions of years passed. Miles of rock were eroded by streams as the land was gradually uplifted. Volcanoes erupted. A land surface devoid of vegetation was sculptured by wind, water, and ice. Centuries went by when the entire region was covered by water. Sediments from the moun-tainous regions of that era buried the Cranberry Gneiss. During one period the southern Appalachian area was submerged beneath a shallow sea similar, perhaps, to the present Gulf of Mexico. By this time more complex forms of life were evolving, and the shells and other remains of countless primitive arthropods settled on the bottom of the sea, forming layers of carbonate rock which in some areas grew to be miles thick. All of these have long since been removed from the Blue Ridge by erosion.

Then, beginning about 450 million years ago, the land mass that was to become North America ground slowly into another great crustal plate. On that plate rode an island chain, or perhaps a continental fragment. The collision occurred first in the southern Appalachian area, then mi-grated northward with time. Sheets of crust up to several miles thick slid slowly over the eastern edge of the continent. The earth's surface crum-pled into folds, fractured, and broke into pieces. Superheated rock and steam melted and altered the sedimentary materials that had been laid down during the previous era. The predecessors of today's Appalachian Mountains were lifted into the prehistoric atmosphere. In the oceans, the first primitive fishes were just evolving.

Some 100 million years later, a similar event occurred: eastern North America once more collided with a continental fragment. Again, the land underwent much uplifting, folding, and breaking apart. More metamorphism took place, and molten rock slipped up fractures into the upper crust.

The third and most recent collision took place 250 to 300 million years ago. This time North America encountered not a continental fragment but the land mass that was to become today's Africa. The southern Appalachian region, especially, witnessed extensive mountain building. For a period of perhaps 50 million years, the continents were fused into one huge land mass. Then they split again, the plates separating pretty much along the seam formed during their collision. The Atlantic Ocean filled the void between the separating land masses, and the southern Appalachians were left essentially as they are today. These last significant events in the formation of the Appalachian Mountains occurred 200 million years ago. The dinosaurs were just beginning their rise to prominence.

This is an overview of how the mountains were uplifted, but that process is only half the story. The Blue Ridge we see is the result not only of creation but of destruction. Erosion—the carrying away of rock material loosened by the forces of wind, water, and chemical decomposition—is the other major factor in the story of mountain formation. You will find the theme familiar: what goes up must come down.

Erosion is one geological process that moves fast enough for visitors to see, at least in a small way. After a good Blue Ridge thundershower, stop along the Parkway where a swollen mountain stream churns beside the road. Scoop up a cupful of water and look carefully at it. Tiny particles will be floating about in suspension, or settling gently to the bottom of your cup. Many of these specks are minute pieces of rock, worn from the summits above you by erosion. Hardly enough, you might think, to affect the height of the mountain—but how many similar cupfuls of water have washed down similar streams in 200 million years? And how much erosion did the ancient forerunners of these mountains undergo? Indeed, the changes wrought in the southern Appalachians through time have been profound.

Rocks are prepared for their trip to the sea by two basic types of weathering: mechanical and chemical. The effects of both can be seen along the Blue Ridge Parkway. Mechanical weathering involves the physical prying-apart of surface rock. Tree roots and even lichens can break down big rocks into smaller pieces. Windblown sand can wear away exposed outcrops. However, the most significant mechanical factor in the southern Appalachians is water, and the most obvious results of water's work can be viewed along the Parkway in the winter and early

3. The forces of mechanical weathering are most active in winter and early spring. Large chunks of fallen rock must often be removed from the road before sections of the Parkway can be reopened.

spring. Wherever rock is exposed, water seeps into its cracks and crevices. Then, when cold weather causes the water to freeze, it expands and splits the rock apart. On south-facing outcrops and road cuts, weathering does its fastest work: on many winter and spring days, the ice melts in the warmth of the sun by late afternoon, only to freeze again after dark. Anyone who has ever used a wedge to split a chunk of wood has simulated this process and witnessed the result. The rock breaks just as does the wood. In some places so much rock falls on the road during the winter that it must be cleared before the Parkway can be reopened for traffic in the spring.

Occasional catastrophic events contribute to physical erosion, as well. Hurricanes (like Camille, which swept across the mountains in August 1969) can dump enough water to cause landslides, moving hundreds of tons of rock and rubble downhill. Evidence of these events can be seen in a number of places along the Parkway: near Reeds Gap (M.P. 13.7), for example, and along the Fallingwater Cascades Trail (M.P. 83.1).

During the warmer months, chemical weathering takes over as the most important agent of rock decomposition. Some of the minerals in rock are soluble in water. In addition, falling rain reacts with various chemicals in the atmosphere to form a mild acid, which helps dissolve elements in the rock even more. As it does so, the rock surface changes chemically—in some ways like a rusting car body—and crumbles away. The results of this process are visible almost anywhere along the Parkway, but some outcrops provide better examples than others. This is because certain rock types (like Cranberry Gneiss) are more subject to chemical weathering than others (like quartzites). Perhaps the most curious result can be seen in the boulders that have formed on the summit of Sharp Top at the Peaks of Otter (M.P. 85.9).

Many of the products of weathering—dissolved minerals and tiny rock fragments—help form the soils of the Blue Ridge. These soils and the plants that grow in them in fact insulate the bare rock and inhibit further erosion. Some of the former rock, though, finds its way into the streams and rivers that drain the mountains, and eventually settles out where they enter the ocean. Indeed, the flat tidewater areas of Virginia and the Carolinas consist of silt, sand, and gravel worn from the southern Appalachians. On their way to the coast, these sediments ground the mountains down further. Carried by rushing floodwaters, rock particles chipped away at the stream bottoms, gradually widening and deepening the beds. In the northern Blue Ridge, water flowing east toward the Atlantic Ocean not only hollowed out the broad Shenandoah, James, and Roanoke River valleys but also wore through the main spine of the mountains in several places. (The James River water gap has already been mentioned.) Further south, streams on the east side of the Blue Ridge province tumble down a steep route to the Atlantic, while those west of the divide follow more leisurely paths to empty eventually into the Gulf of Mexico.

This difference in the steepness of the watercourses has had important consequences for the topography of the southern Appalachians. Streams that drop more abruptly cut into rock more rapidly; therefore, the eastern slopes of the Blue Ridge tend to erode faster. This fact may explain why an imposing escarpment has formed along the eastern side of the province, while most of the western section declines toward flatlands in a gentler way. Occasionally, through the ages, vigorous east-flowing streams have broken through the divide and intercepted sections of the more sluggish west-flowing waters. These "captured" waters then began flowing down the steeper gradients to the east. The Linville River (M.P. 316.6) is an excellent example of a steep watercourse that has cut a deep gorge westward through the escarpment and captured west-flowing streams in the process. And in the Meadows of Dan area of Virginia (M.P. 177.7), this phenomenon—called "stream piracy"—seems destined to occur sometime in the near future ("near" in terms of geological time, that is—it may be centuries). Here, tributaries of the Atlantic-bound Roanoke River are working toward a junction with the Gulf-bound waters of the New River.

The Southern Appalachians Today

The heaving, grinding, wearing forces of the earth have worked for millions of years to produce the views visitors enjoy as they motor along the Blue Ridge Parkway on sunny summer days. Unable to watch the processes of geologic change in the mountains, we can still appreciate their results. Some of the significant geological features of the present-day Appalachians are relatively obvious; others are more obscure but no less interesting.

Invariably, it is the large-scale geology that strikes people first. Visitors familiar with the scenery of the Tetons, the Colorado Rockies, or the Alps may begin by wondering how the less imposing Appalachians qualify as mountains at all. Perhaps their age entitles them to this respect. The Appalachian Mountains are far more ancient than the Alps or the jagged peaks of western North America. Whether or not they ever reached the same lofty heights is hard to establish; some geologists maintain that the Appalachians, too, once surpassed 10,000 feet, but there is no agreement. It is likely, though, that at some point many millions of years ago they were as rugged as the Rockies are now. It is the softening effects of erosion that have through time produced the more worn, rounded topography.

In general, the ridges and summits traversed by the Parkway exist because their rock is more resistant to weathering than surrounding rock types. (The Blue Ridge north of Roanoke gives the visitor a particularly strong sense of this fact.) In weaker strata, water has carved valleys, hollows, and coves. The effects of stream erosion are most spectacularly demonstrated by the James River water gap (M.P. 63.7) and the Linville River gorge (M.P. 316.6). Other impressive examples include the views of Rock Castle Gorge (M.P. 168.7) and the Yadkin River valley (M.P. 289.8). Gaps generally occur at "weak points" in the ridge, particularly where a joint in the rock has permitted water to seep in and erode it.

One large-scale geological feature of the southern Appalachians that goes unnoticed by most visitors is of great interest to geologists. This is the fact that beneath the ancient rock that forms almost all of the visible Blue Ridge province lies a series of *younger* rock layers. Ordinarily, strata are formed in a time sequence, usually as new sediments settle on top of older ones. (The Grand Canyon, for instance, illustrates this kind of layering.) The situation that exists in the southern Appalachians is what one writer describes as "a most disorderly state of affairs, like finding a Neanderthal man buried on top of a Napoleonic soldier."[1] What is the explanation?

Recall that as the mountains were being formed by the collision of crustal plates, large sheets of land slid over adjacent ones. Thus, the

1. Nigel Calder, *The Restless Earth: A Report on the New Geology* (New York: Viking, 1972), 34.

younger rock layers on the surface of one section were trapped underneath the older rock layers on the bottom of the overriding sheet. Millions of years of erosion in the Blue Ridge have worn the upper sheet
down to its oldest strata. Under these, however, lie the younger beds of
the plate beneath. Recent studies indicate that the entire Blue Ridge
province may sit on top of younger rock. North of Roanoke the overlap is
slight, but in North Carolina rocks of the Blue Ridge province have been
pushed dozens of miles west of their original location. Interestingly,
much of the buried younger rock was formed during the time that produced the world's coal, oil, and natural gas, prodding some geologists to
speculate that untapped reserves of fossil fuels may exist miles below the
surface of the southern Appalachians.

There is one place along the Blue Ridge Parkway where visitors can
examine for themselves evidence of this great crustal sliding. In several
areas of the Blue Ridge province, the old rock layers have eroded away
completely, and the younger layers beneath poke through. These holes
are known as "windows," and the Parkway passes through one of the best
known: the Grandfather Mountain window of northwestern North Carolina. The roadway enters the window at about M.P. 284 and leaves it
again at M.P. 316.4. Perhaps the most dramatic view of the "edge" of the
Grandfather Mountain window can be had at Linville Falls (M.P. 316.4).
There, the water plunging over the upper falls pours over a shelf of ancient Cranberry Gneiss, which lies directly on top of rock half a billion
years younger.

Not all the geological features of the southern Appalachians are as
large as entire mountains, drainage systems, or windows. Many smaller
aspects attract visitor attention at overlooks or outcrops along the Blue
Ridge Parkway. Probably the rock types generate the most questions.

Rocks are grouped into three categories according to how they are
formed. *Igneous* rocks are cooled from molten material that wells up to
the surface or solidifies deep within the earth. *Sedimentary* rocks are
formed from sediments that are deposited in layers and later cemented together by their chemical components and by the pressure of overlying
materials and other forces. When rocks of any type are changed in struc-

ture and other characteristics as a result of the extreme heat and pressure they encounter while buried within the earth's crust, they are categorized as *metamorphic*. This is the third group.

There are almost no sedimentary rocks along the Blue Ridge Parkway. Those that do exist here are ancient, and all have been metamorphosed to at least some extent. Since most fossils occur in unmetamorphosed sedimentary rocks younger than 600 million years, it should not be a surprise to discover that there are virtually no fossils found along the Parkway, either. (Sedimentary rocks and fossils do occur in the Alleghany Mountains to the west.)

In fact, almost the entire Blue Ridge province is composed exclusively of igneous and metamorphic rocks. Examples of both groups can be found up and down the Parkway. Igneous granites and charnockites dominate at places like Looking Glass Rock (which can be viewed from M.P. 417.1) and the Peaks of Otter (M.P. 85.9). Pegmatites, veins of igneous rock injected into other types, are common in the Spruce Pine area (M.P. 330.9). Greenstone, originally deposited as an ancient lava flow and then slightly metamorphosed, covers much of the far northern end of the Blue Ridge; it is best seen at Greenstone Overlook (M.P. 8.8). Common metamorphic rocks include gneisses (banded or striated rocks found almost the length of the Parkway), schists, and quartzites. These last are especially noticeable not because of their abundance but because of their great resistance to erosion. Pilot Mountain (seen from M.P. 189.1) is a great block of quartzite, and the dominating height of Grandfather Mountain (M.P. 303) is probably attributable to the fact that it alone among the major Blue Ridge peaks is made of this rock.

Other local features to look for as you travel the Blue Ridge Parkway are layers of different types of rock piled on top of one another, great folds in these rock beds, and cracks or faults where one block has slid against another. All these are prevalent in the southern Appalachians; they are perhaps less noticeable along the Parkway, however, than along other roads—for two reasons. First, few faults and folds appear in Parkway road cuts because for most of its length the Parkway parallels these features rather than cutting across them. And second, where a road cut does expose a fault or fold, it has frequently been obscured: Parkway construction crews, working under the guidance of landscape architects, have blasted out rough, natural-appearing cuts rather than the smooth cross-

4. Aquamarine is one of many gemstones found in the Spruce Pine area. Here, a cut stone is displayed along with the parent rock that produced it.

sectional gaps hewn through the rock for most state and federal highways. Watch carefully as you drive, though. Various formations can be seen in cuts and outcrops by visitors who are observant.

One final element of southern Appalachian geology calls for our attention: the area's minerals and gems. People who have never heard of physiographic provinces or stream piracy scramble over the rubble piles of old mines searching for aquamarine and rubies, or slosh along the edges of mountain brooks picking little flashing specks of gold out of their pans of water and sand. Rock Castle Gorge (M.P. 168.7) was named for the clusters of quartz crystals found in some of its hollows, and various other locations along the Parkway have iron deposits or occasional gems, but "rockhounds" visiting the Blue Ridge Parkway invariably make the Spruce Pine district of North Carolina their main destination.

This area, which extends 25 miles northeast to southwest and is about 12 miles wide, lies immediately west of the Parkway in the area around Gillespie Gap (M.P. 330.9). It has long been renowned for its minerals and gems. Mica, a clear platy material and one of the area's most common minerals, was mined here by native Americans long before European settlers reached the Blue Ridge. In the late 1800s, modern mining began in the Spruce Pine district. Major products through the years have been feldspar (used in pottery and glassmaking), kaolin (a clay employed in the production of fine chinas), and micas (utilized in the electronics industry and many others). The earth has provided other valuable resources, too: quartz, rare earth minerals, asbestos, garnets, and building stone have all been dug here at some time. Today, many people search the old mines for unusual minerals and rock specimens; more than once visitors have stopped me to display emerald-encrusted rocks they had unearthed at one of the area's pay-to-dig mines.

The richness of the Spruce Pine district is due to the unusual number and variety of molten rock veins injected into the area during the mountains' formation. More information about its history and special features is available at the Museum of North Carolina Minerals, located at Gillespie Gap (M.P. 330.9).

5. This truckload of high-quality mica was taken from a mine near
Burnsville, North Carolina in 1955. At that time it was valued at $4,000.

The Effects of Geology on Blue Ridge Life

We have talked much so far about southern Appalachian geology itself, but nothing has been said about how it influences the plants and animals here. Before going on to discuss the flora and fauna, then, a few comments might be appropriate to close this chapter.

Geology has had some general effects on all the things living in the Blue Ridge. You will notice that certain patterns repeat themselves throughout the rest of this natural history guide.

The most important feature of the geology—one that affects all the flora and fauna of the Appalachians—is the height of the mountains. The tall peaks of the southern Appalachians are colder than the surrounding lowlands—drive into the mountains from the Piedmont with your car windows open, and you will notice the temperature drop almost three degrees Fahrenheit for every thousand feet you climb. The mountains are also wetter, for ridges and summits intercept warm, moist winds from the southwest and sweep the water from them. Some places in the southern Appalachian region receive nearly 100 inches of rain a year, making it the second-wettest area in North America (only the Pacific Northwest coast is soggier). Plants and animals must be specially adapted to survive in this environment.

The soil types of the Blue Ridge are dependent to a great extent on the kind of "parent" rock present, and this, too, affects living things. Sandy soils will support different forests and different forest inhabitants than will loamy soils.

Finally, the mere fact that mountain slopes face different directions determines what lives where. A southern slope dries out under the all-day heat of the sun. A high northwest-facing summit endures roaring, icy blasts of prevailing winter winds. Cool waters and a ten-foot thickness of dead leaves collect in a mountain hollow. Different plants and animals exist in each place.

The details of how geology has affected particular plant and animal species appear in following sections. Keep in mind, though, that mountains are what makes the Blue Ridge Parkway special. And, as I hope this chapter has illustrated, geology makes the mountains.

Nonflowering Plants

It has been a rainy spring. Water has soaked the soil and seeped deep into mountain slopes. Somewhere along the Blue Ridge a slice of saturated mountainside lets go, slides down into a hollow, and takes the vegetation and topsoil with it. It sometimes happens: the normally creeping forces of erosion jump with a sudden start, then slow down again.

The warm days of early summer come. The sun beats down on what is now a barren rock slope with a pile of rubble at its base. There are red maples in the nearby forest, and their helicopter seeds blow out into the slide area and settle there. The seeds germinate, but soon—without soil to hold the vital moisture around them—they wither and die. In the mid-afternoon sun the slide area heats up like a sauna, and plants are not welcome there.

The same breezes, though, that wafted the maple seeds to this spot also carried tiny fragments of another living thing—a lichen. Unlike the maple, the lichen is specially adapted to a soilless environment. This tiny piece takes hold and begins to grow, spreading a leathery gray-green crust across the surface of a boulder. Elsewhere in the slide area, other lichens are establishing themselves. Nature's reforestation project—a process called *primary succession*—has begun. And it has begun with a growth few people would even recognize as a plant.

Lichens are considered plants, though. They are grouped in a broad category referred to as the "nonflowering plants." For our purposes, these will include every living thing that doesn't move and doesn't produce flowers. Nonflowering plants can be as simple as one-celled algae or as complex as pine trees. Pines and their relatives are discussed in Chapter 4, but the rest—a diverse bunch forming dozens of strands in the living fabric of the southern Appalachians—are dealt with here.

Lichens

In lichens, Nature has designed living things that can produce their own food, survive in withering sun without moisture for months at a time, and break down solid rock. She has done it, furthermore, as an inventor of true genius might—using parts already on hand.

A lichen is actually a combination of two organisms: a fungus (like mushrooms and bread molds) and an alga (similar to those in lakes and streams). Many kinds of both algae and fungi are found in the southern Appalachians, but they cannot live individually under the scorching sun of boulder fields and stony summits. As a team, however, they can grow almost anywhere. The alga produces food. The fungus—incapable of nourishing itself—utilizes a portion of the alga's food for its survival. In return the fungus may help protect the alga from drying out in the wind and direct sunlight of exposed places.

The resulting combination is a plant that can thrive under the harshest conditions. During long periods of dry weather, lichens shrivel up, maintaining just enough moisture inside to survive. When it rains, they soak up water like blotting paper and spring almost instantly out of their dormancy.

Observant visitors will find many kinds of lichens along the Blue Ridge Parkway. Not all of them are crusty, and not all grow on rocks. Lichens grow on the ground, on fallen logs, and on tree trunks and drape from the branches of firs on the highest mountain summits. Hundreds of species occur in the southern Appalachians; 25 different kinds were found growing on a single split-rail fence at the Peaks of Otter (M.P. 85.9) alone. Most are dull tones of brown, gray, or pale green, but some lure the eye with bright purples, oranges, reds, and yellows.

Though lichens do serve as a source of food for some animals— mites, caterpillars, snails, and slugs are all known to feed on them—their most important role in nature is probably as an agent of erosion. Lichens not only move in to make a new rockslide their home; they help prepare it to be a home for other plants. As a lichen spreads over a rock's surface, it roughens the underlying rock and pries loose tiny particles of it. Hard, erosion-resistant materials like quartzite prevent most lichens from getting a grip, but the softer, grainier rocks that form most of the Blue Ridge can be significantly worn down. In addition to wearing away rocks with their mechanical action, lichens also secrete mild acids that may hasten rock wear. Then, just as happens in weather-caused erosion, minerals and grit collect in cracks and crevices. Pieces of dead lichens, as well as bits of

leaves, twigs, dead insects, and other organic matter borne by the wind from nearby forested areas, also pile up there. Eventually our barren rock slope is ready for the invasion of the next group of specialized plants.

Mosses and Liverworts

Mosses and the closely related liverworts, like the algae, are green plants. Like all green plants they contain the pigment chlorophyll for use in making food. However, several things about them are special among the mountain flora. Unlike terrestrial algae (some kinds of algae do grow by themselves in damp, shady places), mosses and liverworts are leafy-looking. Unlike more advanced species, they do not have a system to transport water and minerals throughout the plant. Instead, nutrients must filter from cell to cell. This "bucket brigade" system, far less efficient than the "firehose" design of higher plants, keeps the size of in-

6. Lichens and mosses are early colonizers of rockslides, and eventually
help produce an environment that less drought-tolerant plants can survive in.

dividual mosses and liverworts small and makes them dependent on abundant moisture. However, it also frees them from a dependence on thick soil. Mosses and liverworts need only the tiniest amounts of nutrients to survive, and for this reason they follow close behind lichens in colonizing rockslides and barren areas.

Liverworts usually grow singly and inconspicuously in damp spots and are of limited importance in the process of succession. Mosses, on the other hand, invade the rocky slope and similar places to form great velvety mats, each one composed of hundreds of moss plants. They also prefer moist locations but, like lichens, can survive long periods of drought. One author tells of a moss kept in a cabinet for 15 years that began to grow again after being wetted.[1]

Mosses carry the reforestation process another step. As they grow, the moss mats thicken. Bottom layers die and rot, adding depth to the soil. Dust and dirt blown by the wind are trapped by the mossy cushions. When rainwater comes, it no longer runs off or evaporates but is held as if by hundreds of sponges in every crack and shady place on the rockslide. Eventually, seeds of more advanced plants land in these natural seed beds, take root, and grow.

Mosses and liverworts form the first of many groups of plants and animals we will talk about that have been affected by the mountains. The many different "miniature environments" in the southern Appalachians provide appropriate conditions for many different kinds. Dry slopes and wet summits, bright ridges and dark coves, different tree species and different soil types all play host to a diverse spectrum of mosses and liverworts. One variety grows almost exclusively in rotting knotholes. Altogether, over 400 species exist in the southern Appalachians – nearly one-third of the total found in North America. Mosses dominate the forest floor at places like Stony Bald (M.P. 402.6) and Richland Balsam (M.P. 431.4), but any overlook or trail will produce its share.

Ferns and Their Allies

Often, the very first plant to spring up from a bed of moss will be a fern. And though lichens and liverworts may escape the notice of visitors

1. Paul M. Patterson, "Woodland Mosses," *Virginia Wildlife* (Feb. 1953).

7. Liverworts, here in the company of a tiny fern, grow best in damp, shady spots.

not familiar with them, ferns in the mountains capture nearly everyone's attention. In some areas they carpet the forest floor with their lacy fronds, making pictures suitable for framing. Ferns also have their own following of enthusiasts: there may not be many moss hunters in the woods, but not a week passes during warm seasons that a Parkway naturalist is not asked how to recognize the southern lady fern common at high elevations, or where to find the curious walking fern.

The fern allies include primitive horsetails and clubmosses. (Some botanists hesitate to call these "fern allies," since they are not in fact that closely related, but the term will do for our purposes.) These inconspicuous plants are relatively uncommon along the Blue Ridge Parkway and fill no unique ecological role; however, as members of plant groups that are hundreds of millions of years old, they serve to remind us of the great age of the Appalachians. Their ancestors grew here in the days of the mountains' infancy.

Ferns and fern allies are considered more advanced than mosses and liverworts, primarily because they have a system to transport water and nutrients throughout the plant. Consequently, they grow to much greater sizes: royal ferns found in some places along the Parkway reach heights of five feet or more. Partly because their transport systems are not as efficient as those of flowering plants, many ferns, horsetails, and clubmosses require fairly moist areas in which to grow. Some of the best places to find them, therefore, are damp woods, stream banks, and other wet spots.

All ferns and their allies, as well as mosses, liverworts, and fungi, reproduce by means of spores. Though similar in purpose to the seeds of higher plants, spores are much different in design. Unlike an acorn, for instance, the spore of a fern has essentially no nutrients in it to help the new plant grow. Unless the spore lands in a very favorable location, it is not likely to germinate successfully. On the other hand, the simplicity of spores allows the fern (or other nonflowering plant) to produce them by the millions. Light as motes of dust, spores are carried for miles by forest breezes. Eventually, a few of them successfully begin the next generation. (For more information on the complex life cycles of many of these plants, see the Suggested Reading list in the back of this book.)

Several dozen kinds of ferns are found along the Blue Ridge Parkway, as well as a handful of clubmosses and horsetails. Many are difficult to tell apart without a field guide, but some are fairly distinctive. Some species are evergreen, and the visitor interested in learning ferns might start in the fall and gain experience with these before the burst of new growth in the spring complicates matters.

Those people who do tramp the woods in November and December are almost sure to encounter Christmas fern. With thick rather than delicate fronds, this dark, shiny green fern is sometimes used in Christmas decorations—hence its name. The visitor who notices that its leaflets are shaped like tiny stockings will find it all the easier to recognize.

The snows and frosts pass, and as the earliest wildflowers bloom in April, new Christmas fern fronds poke up through the dead leaves of the forest floor. Curled up into fuzzy spirals, they are called "fiddleheads." The fiddleheads of other ferns also push up about this time. Another of the common species emerging is the interrupted fern, whose range extends down from the northern states primarily in the mountains. By the time the summer gets into swing, the interrupted fern may be nearly as tall as the five-foot royal fern, its close relative. Its fertile fronds—those that produce the spores of the plant—look as if the middle section of leaflets has been somehow wilted or burned. A closer inspection reveals, though, that it is on these modified parts that the spores are borne.

Various other types of ferns and fern allies grow along the Parkway, each in its own favored habitat. Ground-pine, one of the clubmosses, is generally found in acid soils. Horsetails—leafless, hollow stems reminiscent of bamboo—prefer wet meadows and sandy stream banks. Fragrant hay-scented ferns occur most frequently on bright hillsides and in fields but can grow in many places. The scarce walking fern, in contrast, grows almost exclusively on shaded rock cliffs, preferably those made of limestone. The long, arrowhead-shaped leaves of this unusual fern will root where their tips touch the rock, sending out new leaves and thus "walking" down the rockface. Though limestone cliffs are nonexistent along the Parkway, at least one colony of walking ferns exists in the Rock Castle Gorge (M.P. 168.7), where they are growing on schist.

Mushrooms and Other Fungi

The barren rockslide that began this chapter has passed through the first stages of plant succession: lichens have established themselves, mosses have followed, and ferns and other plants have rooted in the small

8. The "fiddleheads" of the interrupted fern emerge in April. By midsummer its fronds may be over five feet long.

9. Look for the distinctive fronds of maidenhair fern in rich, moist soils.

pockets of soil that built up over time. We can now turn our attention to another group of nonflowering plants: the fungi. Fungi have no chlorophyll and can't produce their own food; therefore, it should not be surprising to learn that they will be found in the greatest numbers where the most food already exists—not on rocky slopes but in mature forests. Rather than wait the centuries it may take for our rockslide community to reach maturity, we'll leave it behind and take a walk into the nearby woods.

Two worlds of fungi exist here in the forests of the Blue Ridge: a visible world and an invisible one. Even the most casual Parkway visitors are familiar with the visible world of fungi—the mushrooms and their close relatives are its major inhabitants, and everyone has seen them. But far more important to the web of life in the mountains is an invisible fungal world that lies under the bark of trees and beneath the leaf litter on the forest floor.

"All students of the fleshy fungi," declares the author of a classic volume on North Carolina flora, "recognize the western moist mountain areas as one of the very richest collecting grounds in North America."[2] Few regions can boast so many varieties of mushrooms. Counting puffballs, morels, cup fungi, coral fungi, shelf fungi, and other mushroom relatives, over 2,000 species have been found in the Great Smoky Mountains National Park alone. The Blue Ridge Parkway undoubtedly provides access to nearly as many kinds.

The richness of the mushroom population of the southern Appalachians results from composite factors. Probably most important is the high amount of rainfall the mountains receive, for fungi thrive in moist surroundings. The great diversity of trees also has a significant effect, as many types of fungi are associated with particular species. The variety of rock types and differences in temperature and elevation from place to place also influence the mushrooms.

Like ferns, fungi have their own following: some Parkway visitors

2. B.W. Wells, *The Natural Gardens of North Carolina* (Chapel Hill: Univ. of North Carolina Press, 1967), 184.

10. Wet weather may not improve vacations, but it does bring on lots of mushrooms, especially in late summer and autumn.

come especially to look for them, photographing or collecting fungi with the same fervor that other people display for watching birds. Many search only for mushrooms that taste good sautéed in butter or batter-fried and served in the company of a steak. Others, not necessarily knowledgeable about fungi, merely enjoy the sight of a group of red-capped *Russulas,* for instance, beaded with the previous night's rain.

There are many notable names in a list of Parkway fungi. Some of the first to emerge during the year, popping up in late April and May, are the morels. These edible fungi (known to Virginia locals as "wood-fish") appear in deciduous forests, especially under tuliptrees and in old apple orchards. They resemble small, stalked sponges; they are fleshy like true mushrooms but not closely related. Morels are probably the most widely eaten wild fungus of all.

Midsummer rains initiate a diverse procession of mushrooms and mushroom cousins. The morels have long since disappeared, but new edibles emerge. Among them are many chanterelles, milk mushrooms, and boletes. Also appearing in midsummer are some of the most poisonous mushrooms in North America: the *Amanitas,* which include the Fly Agaric and the Destroying Angel. These may be found anywhere along the Parkway.

Fungi are found in greatest numbers during late summer and fall, after cool September rains wet the earth; then some of nature's oddities are found. The common stinkhorn, for example, disperses its spores by attracting flying insects with its rank odor, then smearing them with a spore-carrying slime; the slime sticks to the insect, and the spores are thus transported by air to another location. Also appearing in late summer is the jack-o'-lantern mushroom, one of several fungi that glow in the dark. Growing in clusters at the bases of stumps (frequently dead oaks), this mushroom has been found at Fancy Gap (M.P. 199.4), Doughton Park (M.P. 241.1), and Julian Price Park (M.P. 295) and undoubtedly thrives elsewhere as well.

Tremendous numbers of fungi may spring up in certain years. I recall one late summer and autumn when an unusually rainy season in the Blue Ridge had made the forest floor almost soggy. In 15 minutes of looking, even the most half-hearted searcher could find hundreds of mushrooms.

A few words should be added here about collecting mushrooms and other fungi. While the taking of plants, animals, and rocks is not gener-

11. Because they are tasty and easy to identify, morels are the most popular edible mushrooms found in the southern mountains.

ally permitted along the Blue Ridge Parkway, exceptions are made for nuts, berries, other fruits—and mushrooms. The only stipulations are that they must be gathered in small quantities and only for the gatherer's own use. Visitors may feel free, therefore, the sample some of the area's edible fungi.

I would caution you, though, never to feel *too* free about tasting wild mushrooms. Many species native to these mountains are poisonous enough to make a human sick, and several can be deadly. Follow this simple rule: never eat any fungus you are not *certain* is edible. Remember that there is ample room for confusion in identification: professors who have taught classes in fungi for years still find mushrooms they can't identify and must send to specialists. So temper your enthusiasm with a healthy dose of prudence. (Several excellent mushroom handbooks are listed in the back of this volume.)

While you are out in the woods, pick up a handful of dead leaves or roll over an old log. Look underneath, and you will invariably discover a network of white filaments running through the decaying litter of the forest floor. You are getting a glimpse of the invisible world of fungi. Much of that world lies beneath your feet.

It has been estimated that in a year's time up to ten million dead leaves settle on an acre of forest ground. Add to those leaves the wildflowers, twigs, limbs, and dead animals that also fall on that acre, and the total weight of organic matter approaches two tons. It should be apparent that this material does not continue to pile up year after year; rather, it seems to disappear. What actually occurs is that dead plants and animals are broken down and turned into soil. Most of the job is done by those white filaments and their relatives—the fungi of the forest floor.

Some decomposition is, in a sense, the work of mushrooms. As is true of all fungi, mushrooms can't make their own food and so must find it elsewhere. Frequently that food source is dead organic matter. It comes as a surprise to many people that the mushroom itself is only a part of the fungal body. Those white filaments running through the leaf litter are in fact the bulk of the fungus; they give rise to the aboveground parts that we see. Mushrooms and their relatives are only spore-producing bodies connected to extensive networks of food-gathering strands.

In addition, much of the decomposition of dead plants and animals is done by fungi too small to be seen without magnification, but their contribution to mountain communities is on a grand scale. Without their continuous breaking down and releasing of minerals and other substances trapped in dead organisms, the plants of the forests and fields would eventually use up available supplies of nutrients. Life would come to a halt.

Not all fungi receive their nutrition from dead organic material. Many kinds attack living plants and animals; indeed, more plant diseases are caused by fungi than by anything else. The rotting of the heartwood of trees is one example of the effects of fungal disease. The catastrophic chestnut blight (discussed later) was also caused by a fungus. Other varieties attack animals, especially insects: several very specialized types of fungi live solely on the bodies of ants, for example.

Fungi get food in one other way. For a long time, naturalists noticed that certain kinds of mushrooms were found growing under certain species of trees and nowhere else. In recent years it has been discovered that fungi and plant roots in many instances form cooperative structures called "mycorrhizae." In these mutually beneficial associations, fungal tissue surrounds tiny tree rootlets like a sheath. The fungus takes its nourishment from the tree and, in return, appears to help its host obtain nitrogen, phosphorus, and other nutrients ordinarily hard for the tree to absorb. Though this phenomenon needs more study, several things are certain: the tree grows much better in the company of its fungal partner, and many mycorrhizal fungi can't grow at all without a host tree. More and more species of fungi are being found that form these cooperative relationships. Most of them produce mushrooms.

Bacteria

Many scientists maintain that fungi are so different from other non-flowering plants that they should be grouped in a different category. Others are not so sure. Bacteria, though, are almost universally separated from plants, and we will consider them here only for the sake of convenience.

Many readers may wonder why bacteria are mentioned at all. Most people associate bacteria in their daily lives only with disease, and visitors may figure that the only microorganisms likely to be of significance along the Blue Ridge Parkway are the ones that infect their children's throats in the middle of a vacation. However, many bacteria play important

—though unseen—roles in nature. Some do cause disease—in plants and animals as well as humans. A large number are involved, like fungi, in the breakdown and decomposition of dead plant and animal materials. Indeed, if we could count all the individual organisms living in an acre of litter on the forest floor, bacteria would account for 40 percent of them (second only to the fungi's 50 percent). In addition, bacteria—again like some fungi—form cooperative relationships with other organisms (even humans: they aid in digestion, for example). Perhaps best known is the association between certain bacteria and plants of the legume or pea family. Here, in exchange for nutrients, the bacteria manufacture nitrogen compounds needed for growth by their hosts. In fact, the bacteria produce more nitrogen compounds than their host plant needs. The farmer who wishes to make use of this excess to fertilize his fields naturally will plant alfalfa or clover. Some wild members of the pea family flourish in the forests of the southern Appalachians.

In general, nonflowering plants probably receive less attention from visitors than any other flora or fauna along the Blue Ridge Parkway. In some ways, though, visiting any park or natural area is like attending a theatrical play: the people the audience notices most—the actors—are not the only ones who have made important contributions to the production. Behind the set, above the stage, and elsewhere out of sight are many necessary participants who are rarely acknowleged by the audience. But to comprehend the whole show—or the whole natural world—even vaguely, we have to understand their roles a bit, too.

Wildflowers

For millions of years, nonflowering plants blanketed the earth. In the huge swamps that covered much of the North American continent before the era of dinosaurs, ferns thrived, and forests of giant clubmosses grew 100 feet tall. Later, ancestors of today's cone-bearing trees evolved, becoming common at the same time that the earliest mammals were appearing.

Somewhere in this procession of centuries, somewhere in these primeval forests, plants first began to put forth flowers. The blooms may have looked something like present-day magnolias. Primitive beetles fumbled from blossom to blossom, attracted by the scent of possible food, and inadvertently carried pollen that was to fertilize hundreds of eggs. In the process, beetles helped to establish a group of flora that would eventually come to dominate the earth—the flowering plants.

People commonly think of "flowering plants" as those that appear in gardens and greenhouses, spring woods and summer fields. However, the group also includes weeds, grasses, sedges, and in North America nearly all shrubs and trees except pines and their relatives. All these have flowers—some are just more conspicuous than others. And while it is true that under special environmental conditions nonflowering plants are still the most common types, it can safely be said that flowering plants are supreme throughout the world.

The current dominance of flowering plants is the result of evolution, nature's constant effort to match organisms to changing environmental conditions. (Or, as a handyman might say, to use the right tool for the job.) Ferns, horsetails, and clubmosses, for instance, were ideally suited to populate wetlands. Groups that evolved as the earth's climate changed produced a new set of survival characteristics. One of the most important was a means of sexual reproduction that worked on dry land. Sexual reproduction—which allows for the mixing of characteristics from two parents—provides for a greater diversity of traits in a population and therefore a better chance that at least some members of the species will survive even if living conditions should change. Sexual reproduction is, in short, a sort of survival insurance. The lower plants all need water to

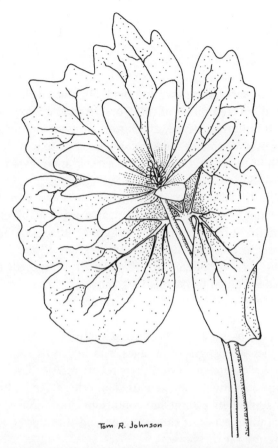

Tom R. Johnson

carry on sexual reproduction; little wonder that they flourished only in prehistoric swamps. Cone-bearing trees evolved a system that operates without water: they produce pollen, sexual cells that drift on air currents rather than swim through liquid. The windborne pollen grains land by chance on receptive cells of other plants of the same species and fertilize them. Armed with this innovation and an improved water transport system, cone-bearing plants began the colonization of the earth's increasingly drier environments.

Every spring, though, they paid a price for their pioneering. In order to ensure that their reproductive system worked successfully, every primitive pine and spruce had to produce tremendous quantities of pollen. For every grain that managed to pollinate another tree, thousands more ended their windblown travels in rock crevices, mudflats, or primeval lakes. For the plant, it was pollen and energy wasted.

What improved system might evolve that would be more efficient? Eventually, the flowering plants provided an answer. Rather than relying on capricious breezes to carry their pollen, flowering plants enlisted insects to do the job. Waste was cut dramatically—pollen was no longer broadcast randomly into the air but transferred directly from blossom to blossom. The flowering plants also developed a tremendous number of seed dispersal techniques. They produced seeds that fly, seeds that float, seeds that hitch rides with passing animals, and countless other variations. They evolved a system of water-conducting vessels even more efficient than the smaller tracheids of the cone-bearing plants. Gradually these versatile foodmaking machines—the flowering plants—outcompeted and replaced other plant groups all over the earth. From what was probably only a handful of ancestors, they have evolved and diverged into more than 250,000 different kinds worldwide.

The southern Appalachian region supports a healthy share of this diversity. In the Great Smoky Mountains, regarded as the botanically richest area of the southern mountains, nearly 1,400 varieties are found. A preliminary study listed over a thousand species of flowering plants occurring along the Blue Ridge Parkway, and a later research team notes that "if this list were eighty percent complete" the Parkway environs would be home to nearly as many kinds of plants as the Smokies.[1]

The tremendous diversity of the southern Appalachian flora has drawn botanists here for as long as there have been students of science in North America. The self-taught naturalist John Bartram of Philadelphia visited the area in the days before the Revolutionary War, collecting plants new to eighteenth-century science and sending seeds and specimens to friends in England. (Though Bartram stayed mainly in the valleys, he approached at least as close as Natural Bridge, Virginia—today a short drive from the James River Visitor Center, M.P. 63.6.—to the present Parkway site.) Bartram's son William penetrated even deeper into the southern mountains, which in 1775 still constituted a wilderness hundreds of footsore miles from civilization. Other famous botanists who

---

1. J. Dan Pittillo and Thomas E. Govus, *Important Plant Habitats of the Blue Ridge Parkway* (National Park Service Report, 1978), 5.

have tramped the Blue Ridge and its neighboring ranges searching for new plants include André and François Michaux, Thomas Nuttall, and Asa Gray.

For today's botanists and wildflower enthusiasts, the Parkway provides easy access to many mountain habitats that at one time could be reached only by great expenditure of energy and sweat. Thousands of people come to see the spectacular blooming of azaleas, rhododendrons, and mountain laurel in late spring; the mountains have a reputation for grandeur at this time. Even casual observers will note, though, that every month of the growing season has its own assortment of blossoms. You could travel the Parkway's full length weekly from March until November and not catalog them all.

Flowers through the Seasons

"Spring fever" is the affliction that sends naturalists and wildflower buffs out into the woods as soon as the sunlight is strong enough to turn lingering ice and snow into mud. The first good thaw usually finds sections of the Blue Ridge Parkway still closed, but visitors – mostly local people – come searching for signs of spring nonetheless. Finding the year's first wildflower is always a triumph.

The first plant to appear in the spring actually melts its way up through the cold ground. Skunk cabbage, found in swampy areas, generates heat as it grows and usually pushes up before any other spring plants. In places like Rock Castle Gorge (M.P. 168.7), the odd, enclosed flower spike of skunk cabbage may bloom as early as late January; even in cold years it is out by the first of March. However, since it is neither common along the Parkway nor particularly showy, this first sign of spring usually goes unnoticed by visitors.

The wildflower season does not begin in earnest until a later date, determined chiefly by elevation. Like a slowly incoming tide, warm weather reaches valley floors first, then rolls gradually up the slopes. The delicate bloodroot is one of the next wildflowers to bloom; it may appear in low elevations at Rock Castle Gorge and around the James River (M.P. 63.6) in mid-March, but it is likely to be the first or second week of April before bloodroot blossoms along the Boone Fork Trail at Cone-Price (M.P. 297), several thousand feet higher.

Although this variance in bloom times makes it difficult to tell inquiring visitors when to come to see certain flowers, it does have advantages. If you missed springtime near Asheville (M.P. 384) you might still catch it at Craggy Gardens (M.P. 364.6), only a half-hour's drive away. And visitors returning to the North after a winter in Florida can experience a month's worth of spring flora in a week along the Blue Ridge Parkway.

Joining bloodroot in the early spring are a number of other fairly common woodland wildflowers. Spring beauty, hepatica, Dutchman's-breeches, squirrel corn, and a number of different kinds of violets—in purples, blues, yellows, and whites—all appear in April. Great or star chickweed (a relative of the chickweed that plagues lawn owners) carpets large areas with its small white flowers. False hellebore comes up in wet spots and along stream banks; though it doesn't bloom until early summer, the large pleated leaves of this plant attract a lot of attention and are the subject of many visitors' questions.

The days grow slightly warmer; early spring slides into midspring; and many of the earliest flowers fade, to be replaced by new species. Among the showiest of these are trilliums. The large-flowered trillium grows the length of the Parkway and in some areas (like Humpback Rocks, M.P. 5.8, and Crabtree Meadows, M.P. 339.5) covers the forest floor with its lilylike white flowers. The red erect trillium (or wake-robin) and the painted trillium also emerge in late April and May. Crested dwarf irises with their large lavender blossoms, columbines, and brilliant red fire pinks are other conspicuous wildflowers appearing at this time.

The display of color around your feet in spring is matched overhead by the blooms of a number of southern Appalachian trees. The first to attract attention is the serviceberry or "sarvis," a small tree present along most of the Parkway. The appearance of its plentiful white blossoms soon after the melting of winter's snow was said in the mountains to signal the arrival of the traveling preacher, who would hold the spring's first "sarvis."

Another tree conspicuous in April is one called royal paulownia, or princess tree, an import from Asia. The princess tree is not found in the middle of the forest but can be seen along road banks and elsewhere near human populations. Its purple flowers catch the eye of visitors along the Parkway in the area of Roanoke, Virginia, and farther south, from M.P. 380 to M.P. 400. Also appearing in limited areas about this time is red-

12. Many trees bloom in the spring. Silverbell is found along the southern stretches of the Blue Ridge Parkway.

bud. In parts of the piedmont and lower elevations of the Smokies, this small, pink-flowered tree is very common. On the Parkway, though, it is generally restricted to the Roanoke (M.P. 110) and James River (M.P. 63.6) areas.

Much more prevalent is the flowering dogwood, state flower of both North Carolina and Virginia. This small tree begins to bloom at lower elevations in mid-April but does not come into full prominence until May. Then it can be seen throughout deciduous woods up to about 5,000 feet, decorating the slowly greening forest with white and pale pink. Right on its heels the Fraser magnolia (first discovered by William Bartram) puts forth its huge, pale yellow flowers. It is found from Rocky Knob (M.P. 169) south, generally at lower elevations.

The last trees to bloom along the Parkway do so after all the leaves have emerged. Black locust grows mainly in young forests, producing showy white flowers in mid-May. The tuliptree, a member of the magnolia family, blooms at about the same time. The large cream and orange blossoms give the tree its name. (It is also called tulip poplar or yellow poplar.) By mid-June the waxy petals have dropped off and showered down on the forest floor.

Through these same sunny days of late spring, dozens of other wildflowers hurriedly bloom and wilt. Plants like bluets, phlox, galax, yellow sundrops, and showy goat's-beard are all common along roadsides. Many rarer plants blossom in places discovered only by the knowledgeable and the lucky. Among them are pink and yellow ladyslippers, showy orchis, and prickly-pear cactus.

As spring glides into summer, the mountains' most spectacular floral exhibition builds to a crescendo. The heath family in the southern Appalachians includes a number of colorful shrubs, and these bloom in a crowded sequence during May and June. First in early May, comes pinxter-flower, a pink azalea found occasionally in the woods along most of the Parkway. About the same time, flowers of the uncommon Carolina rhododendron emerge, especially on the cliffs of Linville Gorge (M.P. 316.4). Mid-May adds the brilliant yellows and oranges of the flame azalea. Found only sporadically north of Roanoke (the Humpback Rocks

13. Black birch is one of a number of wind-pollinated trees found in the Blue Ridge. Like most of them, its flowers are very inconspicuous.

14. Showy orchis displays its lavender and white blossoms in April.

Picnic Area, M.P. 8.5, is a good spot), the flame azalea lines the roadsides in areas near Rocky Knob (M.P. 169), Craggy Gardens (M.P. 364.6), and Mount Pisgah (M.P. 408.6). A view of this shrub on a sunny day is convincing evidence that its name is an apt one.

It is generally early June when catawba or purple rhododendron begins to bloom. Next to the arrival of autumn colors, no single event brings so many visitors to the Blue Ridge Parkway. Blooming occurs in the woods around the Peaks of Otter (M.P. 85.9) about the first week of the month. Less than a week later, the bushes in the Doughton Park area (M.P. 241.1) reach their peak. The climax, however, comes around June 20: it is then that the rhododendrons bloom at Craggy Gardens (M.P. 364.6).

Those who have not visited any of the rhododendron "balds" of the southern Appalachians at this time of year may find it difficult to visualize such a spectacle. At Craggy Gardens—where the trees are small and sparse, and do not obscure the view—acres of rhododendron bushes cover several summits and their intervening ridges. In a good bloom year, they are covered with great bunches of pink and purple flowers, forming an almost unbroken carpet of color; even in a poor season, the display is remarkable.

Rhododendrons are still blooming when mountain laurel produces its delicate pink and white blossoms. In some spots the flowering of the mountain laurel can be nearly as showy as that of its larger cousin. In early July those at Craggy Gardens and other high elevations begin to brown at the edges and drop to the ground, but one last member of the group, the white or rosebay rhododendron, puts forth its array of flowers through about the third week of July, usually a subtler echo of the previous month's events. Then these fade, as well. It is the end of the Parkway's most vibrant floral show.

Occasionally, visitors from outside the southern Appalachian area become confused about which members of this group of flowers they are seeing. The problem is not in telling them apart; though all are heaths (along with wintergreen and blueberries), each has fairly obvious distinguishing characteristics. The problem is that local people and the guidebooks call these plants by different names. Catawba rhododendron becomes "purple laurel," and rosebay rhododendron is "big laurel" (because the shrubs are larger); mountain laurel is "ivy," and azalea "honeysuckle."

15. Visitors travel miles to see catawba rhododendron bloom at Craggy Gardens in late June. The intensity of the display varies from year to year.

Wildflowers

To the visitor uncertain about flowers to begin with, a conversation with a mountain resident can be very confusing. Cultivate the attitude that names are not important, though, and you will find that rhododendrons can be enjoyed without labels.

By midsummer, forest wildflowers have for the most part finished blooming. Sourwood trees produce their graceful clusters of nectar-laden blossoms in July, and some of the mountains' rare orchids bloom in summer (the Parkway is home to nearly 30 members of this family), but the great diversity of the spring flora is noticeably absent from the woods.

In fields and pastures, though, and along roadsides and fencerows, flowers pop up everywhere. The hot summer sun brings out acres of ox-eye daisies and black-eyed Susans, yellow hawkweeds, delicate yarrow, and Queen Anne's lace. From Rockfish Gap to Cherokee, various field flowers line the roadway from June on.

Some varieties particularly arrest visitors' attention. In July the lilies bloom—not only the common orange day lily, first brought to the mountains by early settlers, but rarer kinds as well. Gray's lily, found in meadows from Smart View (M.P. 154.5) to Craggy Gardens (M.P. 364.6), is a nationally threatened species found only in the southern Appalachians.

A group that might be referred to as "butterfly plants" also grow thickly in many spots. They produce quantities of nectar and, as a result, attract insects in swarms. Bright orange butterfly weed is one of the most showy, appearing prominently in fields near the James River (M.P. 63.6) and Doughton Park (M.P. 241.1) in July. Other notable species are common milkweed, Joe-Pye weed, ironweed, and boneset. All are found in fields and along the roadside.

As Labor Day approaches, many of the plants that have bloomed earlier in the season begin to distribute their seeds. The observant visitor will find all sorts: winged seeds, downy plumed seeds from hawkweeds, pea-like redbud pods. There are also various berries, many of which have a special attraction for people who appreciate wild edibles. Mountain blackberries and blueberries ripen in late summer, and collecting and enjoying them along the Parkway is permitted.

Some of the season's last wildflowers are in bloom as school-children get ready to return to their classrooms. Jewelweed (also called snapweed or touch-me-not), taking over wet areas and stream banks, is in flower, and white snakeroot fills the woods. Numerous varieties of goldenrod and aster decorate the Parkway in August and September, many blooming until the first frost.

The final plant to bloom in the fall, like the first to flower in the spring, is obscure and easily overlooked. Witch-hazel, a small tree found intermittently throughout the southern Appalachian deciduous woods, puts forth its stringy yellow blossoms after the leaves have already fallen from its limbs—sometimes even after the first snowfall. The faint tangerine smell of witch-hazel is autumn's last floral scent. The wildflowers will be dormant now until spring.

Wildflowers from Another Perspective

The attractiveness of wildflowers is enough for them to merit our interest and appreciation. However, flowers are more than colorful additions to the roadside scenery—nature, after all, did not produce them just to please human eyes. Flowers have another purpose: they insure that the seeds produced to begin the next generation will bear a new mixture of plant traits. As the structures of sexual reproduction in plants, flowers are all business. They bloom, exchange their pollen with other blossoms of the same type, and then wither as the plant produces seed—the product of their efforts. Much of what we appreciate about wildflowers is in fact important to this biological process.

Look closely, for instance, at a rhododendron blossom. The same purple color that draws the human eye also attracts bees. Moreover, even the dainty brown spots on the petal directly above the flower's center have a purpose: they form an incoming bee's target, its "landing lights," and insure that the bee will successfully pollinate the flower. The bee, in return, receives nectar as a reward—and as an incentive to fly on to another rhododendron blossom.

This exchange represents only one of many relationships that exist between wildflowers and other members of the southern Appalachians' natural community. Like everything else in nature, flowers contribute to the complex web of life here. If you know what to look for, you can spot other examples of these interactions. It is not hard, for instance, to pick out other wildflowers that are pollinated by bees. You need only know a few things about bees: they can see some colors, for example, but red looks like gray to them. It may not be a surprise to discover, therefore, that most bee flowers are blue, yellow, white, or purple. (Interestingly, some flowers have markings that reflect ultraviolet light—invisible to us, but attractive to bees.) In addition, many have patterns of spots or lines similar to those on the rhododendron blossom. Called "honey guides," these targets can be seen on violets and foxgloves. Bees also have a keen sense of smell, and many bee flowers attract them with very pleasant fragrances.

Some types of flowers are pollinated by flies; these, too, have distinctive smells. It is a different sort of odor that attracts a fly, however, and not surprisingly, fly-pollinated flowers are not generally found in gardens or florist shops. Many smell like rotting meat. They are also drab in appearance, and this fact coupled with their relative scarcity in the Blue Ridge cloaks them in obscurity.

In the southern Appalachians, a number of plants depend upon hummingbirds to carry their pollen. Since birds have virtually no sense of smell, hummingbird flowers are scentless. The color vision of birds, on the other hand, is excellent. Most hummingbird flowers are red or orange, wavelengths of light that attract birds yet do not draw bees (the structure of the blossom is such that bees might steal nectar without pollinating the flower). Cardinal-flower and columbine are both examples of hummingbird-pollinated flowers found along the Parkway. Watchful visitors will spot additional ones.

Logic may lead you to the discovery of other pollinators as well. Does a particular flower open only in the evening? Perhaps it is visited by moths. Are the flower parts of another blossom tough and waxy? The plant probably relies on beetles to carry its pollen, clumsy insects that might damage a more delicate bloom. Have you encountered a plant whose flowers lie on the ground? It may be pollinated by ants.

Some flowers are "generalists": they attract all kinds of pollinators and have no special structures or designs. Common milkweed is one of these (see Chapter 6 for more about the insects associated with this plant). Other flowers, however, have evolved such complex relationships with specific pollinators that they seem to have been lifted from the pages of science fiction.

16. The dark lines or "honey guides" on the lower petal of the northern white violet present a target for incoming bees.

Wildflowers

Among the best examples to be found along the Blue Ridge Parkway is the yellow ladyslipper. The lower petal is modified to form a hollow pouchlike structure that gives the flower its name. Inside the blossom a sweet odor is produced, which attracts one of only several kinds of burrowing bees. The bee lands on the lip of the pouch, slips off its slick surface, and tumbles inside. The insect is trapped: the design of the flower prevents it from getting out the way it got in. However, there is another escape route. Thin translucent membranes in the back of the pouch let light in, and draw the bee just as sunny windows draw insects trapped in a house. At the back of the flower the insect finds a passageway up and out. On its way, though, it drops onto the anthers of the flower. A sticky wad of pollen adheres to the bee's back (conveniently out of its reach). The bee escapes, flies off, and eventually lands on another ladyslipper. There, it falls in once again. This time, the escaping bee deposits its cargo of pollen on the stigma, and the flower is pollinated.

There are a few flowering plants that no animal pollinates. In fact, many people do not realize that they flower at all. These species rely, like cone-bearing plants, on the wind. Many southern Appalachian trees are in this category. Their flowers are unattractive and insignificant: no bright petals, no intricate shapes, no pleasant scents. For a plant that depends on wind, all those features would be costly and useless extras. Indeed, large, showy flowers would only get in the way of the pollen. Since it is to the tree's advantage to have its pollen blown about as freely as possible, not only do wind-pollinated varieties have reduced flowers, but they almost all bloom before their leaves fully emerge, dumping thousands of pollen grains into the air in early spring. The cost in extra pollen is apparently countered by the savings in elaborate flowers and nectar. In any event, wind-pollinated trees—oaks, most maples, birches, and others—thrive in the mountains.

As "foreigners" in the southern Appalachian woods, we humans see things from a different perspective than do the land's animal residents. A violet to us is a delicate wildflower that blooms in the early spring, then disappears. The bee is also interested in the flower, but as a source of food rather than inspiration. And many animals rely on the plant without giving the bloom special attention. To the caterpillar of a fritillary butterfly, the violet is a cluster of green leaves, the insect's sole source of food throughout its larval life. The ecological importance of many other forest

60

plants, too, goes well beyond the role their flowers play. The catbird relies on the fruit of the wild strawberry to feed its newly hatched young. A cottontail rabbit dashes into a tangle of blackberry canes to dodge a pursuing fox. Deer find moisture during a hot, dry August by browsing on succulent jewelweed.

Because of the great diversity of flowering plants in the southern Appalachians, the complexity of their interactions with other elements of nature is fantastic. The diversity of wildflowers is apparent to anyone who visits the Blue Ridge Parkway during the growing season, which is a dazzling eight-month-long parade of shapes and hues and fragrances. This is the beauty of the artist. But another sort of beauty appeals to the skilled mechanic, a beauty not of form but of function. An appreciation of either one will add to the pleasures of a stay in the southern Appalachians. An appreciation of both will bring with it a greater realization of why the natural communities of these mountains have been preserved.

Trees

Leaves begin to appear on southern Appalachian trees in April. This most important event of the spring happens so quickly that we often miss it. We look one morning, and the young oak leaves are as big as mouse ears; the next time we notice them, they are as big as mice. "It seems like only last week there was snow on the ground," we say, "and here it is practically summer."

Some schoolchildren become sensitive to this change in the forest. Their teachers have instructed them to choose one leaf and watch it grow. The students trace the outline of their leaf every day, then they compare their drawings to see the increase in its size as time passes. And if the teacher is a knowledgeable naturalist and the children observant enough, the class discovers that all of nature is acutely responsive to the leafing out of the trees. Insects rouse from their winter dormancy, and the further the leaves emerge, the more the insects seek them out for food and protection. Birds begin to build nests where the leaf cover has grown thick enough to hide them.

On the forest floor, wildflowers are also reacting: the bigger the leaves grow on the trees, the fewer wildflowers bloom. The class may measure this trend by counting the number of blossoms in a marked area from week to week. Why are the wildflowers disappearing? Perhaps each time the class visits the nearby woodlot, the teacher uses a light meter to measure the amount of sunlight reaching the forest floor. Someone eventually figures it out: most wildflowers need the full energy of bright sunshine to grow and bloom. As a result, many pass through their entire aboveground life cycles before emerging tree leaves throw the forest floor into shade. At lower elevations, the bountiful woodland wildflower display ends by late May. Spring sweeps rather slowly up the southern Appalachian slopes, but by mid-June flowers at even the highest elevations are in full retreat below the thickening forest canopy. The woods are green once more.

The Blue Ridge Parkway is 469 miles long, and come summer every mile of it is green. Views from overlooks are vast expanses of green. Visitors spreading out picnics, setting up camping trailers, or strolling down

17. Once their buds break, leaves emerge rapidly, requiring only a week or two to become full sized.

woodland paths encounter no color more prominent. And every green leaf, frond, and blade of grass should read like a sign: "Food made here."

The green color we see is the pigment chlorophyll. Chlorophyll enables every green plant to harness the sun's energy, then use that energy to alter water and carbon dioxide chemically, converting them into oxygen and simple sugars. The oxygen is released into the atmosphere; it is merely a by-product of this process of photosynthesis. The simple sugars and other products of photosynthesis become roots, stems, leaves, branches, trunks, flowers, fruits — and the basis of existence for every form of animal life in the forest.

In the forests of the southern mountains (as in almost all forests), it is the trees that contain the most food. Were we to uproot all the plants on an acre of forest land and carry them to our laboratory, for every load of wildflowers, shrubs, and ferns we transported, we would need to haul dozens of piles of tree leaves, tree limbs, tree trunks, and tree roots. And since trees contain the most food, they play the dominant role in feeding the forest's animal life.

Just how big is that role? A casual walk through the woods may lead a visitor to the conclusion that not very much plant material gets used by other organisms. After all, one doesn't encounter the stumps of trees that have been entirely eaten, or great bare areas where some hungry animal has satiated a vast appetite. But look closer. Try to find a single leaf that does not have at least one hole chewed into it; in June this may not be a formidable task, but by September it is likely to be difficult indeed. Or locate a white oak tree and search beneath it for one of last year's acorns. You will probably discover that the deer, squirrels, chipmunks, and mice have already been exceptionally thorough.

Dead plant materials as well as live ones feed the animal inhabitants of the forest. When autumn leaves, old branches, and entire dead trees fall to the ground, insects, millipedes, worms, fungi, and bacteria throng to this new food supply. By the time the life-and-death cycle of a tree is completed, forest organisms have consumed every last particle.

Trees, with assistance from other green plants, form the solid foundation of all life in the southern Appalachians. Even animals that do not seem to have the slimmest connection to trees depend upon them, for the mouse that fed the snake that fed the red-tailed hawk survived until its last moment by eating acorns and the bark of young twigs. And as in any

18. Because trees and other green plants can convert light into food, they form the vital link between animals and the sun's energy.

type of construction, the kind of foundation dictates the sort of structure that can be built on top of it. In the southern Appalachians, the geology has provided for a number of different forest types. This means, in turn, that all sorts of natural communities—with a tremendous diversity of living things—are based on these forest types.

It is difficult to overstate the importance of trees in the natural history of the mountains, for trees greatly determine not only the kinds but the character of life here. It can even be legitimately claimed that trees put the "Blue" in Blue Ridge, for hydrocarbons released into the atmosphere by the forest contribute to the characteristic haze on these mountains and to their distinctive color.

A Variety of Forest Types

Different trees, like different people, prefer different sorts of weather. Consequently, temperature and rainfall are essential variables that help determine where certain kinds of trees will grow well. In the mountains the average temperature and annual rainfall (along with the related levels of soil moisture) are determined, in turn, by the geology. Thus the composition of the southern Appalachian forests is determined by several basic facts.

The most important of these is that the higher you go, the colder it gets; summers on the highest summits are cool and winters quite cold. Altitude in effect alters the whole climate of a given area. In Asheville (M.P. 382.4) the average high temperature during the year is 67.5°F; on Mount Mitchell (M.P. 355.3) it is only 51.1°F. Some trees do well in cold weather and are found at high elevations; some don't and aren't.

Another trend, though not as predictable, is that annual precipitation also increases with elevation. Along the Virginia section of the Parkway, difference in rainfall between the Blue Ridge summits and the nearby piedmont areas may amount to only a few inches a year. In North Carolina, however, the difference is often more substantial: the Asheville area receives about 40 inches of precipitation annually, while the section of Parkway near Mount Hardy (M.P. 422.8) may get more than 80 inches. Also important is how much of the precipitation falls as snow. Although Mount Mitchell has only about twice as much annual precipitation as Asheville, it averages five to six times more snow—60 inches, compared with 11 inches Asheville residents shovel each winter. Trees that live at high elevations must be able to either stand up under the weight of this snow or shed it, which not all species are designed to do.

Topography, too, has important effects on the forest. Slopes that face south may bake under the sun from morning till evening, thereby losing much of their soil moisture by evaporation. As a result, they are drier than the shaded north-facing slopes, even though both may receive the same amount of rain. Similarly, water runs quickly off the ridgetops, but hollows collect it; during a dry summer, there may be twice as much moisture in cove soils as in the soil on nearby summits. Different forest types are found in each of these areas.

Finally, various qualities of the soil influence the forest. For example, soils derived from quartzite tend to be sandy, provide fewer nutrients, and hold less water than those produced from feldspar-rich rocks. Because the patterns of bedrock in these mountains are complex, so are the patterns of soils.

As the previous chapter pointed out, there is a wide diversity of flowering plants in the southern Appalachians. Among this assortment are more than 100 kinds of flowering trees—nearly as many as in all of Europe—plus 14 native conifers. However, despite the number of species, most of the forests along the Blue Ridge Parkway can be separated into a few types, each dominated by just a handful of the more common trees. These forest groupings overlap and grade into one another like colors in a rainbow, in defiance of our arbitrary definitions and boundaries. As with the bands of the spectrum, though, it is easiest to talk about them as distinct units.

Forests of Lower Elevations

The most common forest the Blue Ridge Parkway passes through is the *oak-chestnut* forest. Its dominant trees are oaks: white, northern red, black, scarlet, and chestnut oak are all found in one place or another (all five occur at Porter's Mountain Overlook, M.P. 90). Many other kinds of trees appear occasionally. Depending on conditions at a particular site, one may find red maple, any of several hickories, white pine, sourwood, black locust, black walnut, and (in wetter spots) both eastern hemlock and American beech.

One of the trees you will not find is the American chestnut. Given that circumstance, it may seem odd to call this forest "oak-chestnut." However, there was a time when the chestnut not only grew in these woods but was the single most common tree species rooted in the southern Appalachian soil. In the oak-chestnut forest it commonly made up 40 percent of the trees; in some spots chestnuts grew in almost pure stands. Fallen nuts fed generations of squirrels, bears, deer, and wild turkeys, and wagonloads were collected by mountain people to fatten hogs, feed families, and use as an item of trade. In addition, the logs, almost impervious to rot, made fine cabins and outbuildings.

But that was 100 years ago. Not long before the turn of the century, a fungus called the chestnut blight entered this country, the result of an innocent human mistake. It was so inconspicuous an event that no one is sure exactly how and where the fungus arrived; most likely, it was carried by some Chinese chestnut trees that were imported by a New York botanical garden.

It was perhaps five years before anyone was even aware that a new tree disease was loose in the United States. In the early 1900s, dying American chestnuts were discovered at the Bronx Zoo and in nearby New Jersey. The fungus was isolated and identified, but it was already too late. The blight swept through the forests of the Northeast, then down the Appalachian chain. It was impossible to stop the spread of its spores: some, as light as particles of dust, dispersed in the breezes; others adhered to birds and insects that landed on infected trees. The spores entered healthy trees through wounds in the bark, growing into a new fungal body that clogged the plants' tissues and effectively choked them to death.

Various control methods were tried—both scientific attempts and the crudest of home remedies—but none proved an effective cure. The chestnut blight moved south and west, wiping out the vast chestnut component of the eastern forests. In 1918, the fungus struck the Peaks of Otter area (M.P. 85.9); in the early and middle 1920s, it decimated trees around Rocky Knob (M.P. 169); by 1930, 80 to 90 percent of the chestnuts in western North Carolina were infected. It appeared that the American chestnut was well on its way to extinction.

The disappearance of one of its major trees had a profound effect on the southern Appalachian forest community. An important source of food for many animals was entirely eliminated, and the numbers of some spe-

19. Stark skeletons of dead American chestnut trees haunted the woods along the Parkway into the 1960s. Most have since fallen.

cies were undoubtedly reduced. Several kinds of insects that had been associated with the chestnut did not survive. Great gaps were opened in the forest canopy, and throngs of new plants sprouted up from the forest floor. The mountains were radically changed.

It should be noted that the chestnut was not completely exterminated. The root systems of the trees survived the blight and have periodically sent up new shoots ever since. These young chestnut trees are common in some places along the Parkway and elsewhere; some occasionally grow large enough to bear a crop of nuts. The chestnut blight is still present, though, and inevitably these new sprouts contract it and are strangled out of existence. Research continues in an attempt to defeat the fungus; hopes have been raised with the discovery that certain viruses weaken some strains of the blight, but there have been no breakthroughs that would return the American chestnut to its former dominance.

Until ecologists can learn how the oak-chestnut forest type will adjust to the loss of the chestnut, most will probably continue to use its current name. So far, oaks and hickories have filled the gaps left by the blight. Variations of these oak and oak-hickory woods can be found at moderate elevations along the entire Blue Ridge Parkway. Some of the best examples are just south of the James River (at M.P. 68), along the Smart View Trail (M.P. 154.5), and at Chestoa View (M.P. 320.8).

Wherever damp soils are found at low and middle elevations (as in protected coves and hollows), the oak-chestnut forest blends into another type: the *cove hardwoods* forest. It is here that the southern Appalachians produce the greatest variety of trees in any one spot. A single cove forest may be populated by over 40 species, and some in the Great Smoky Mountains (where the richest cove hardwood stands are found) have many more.

It is hard to pick the dominant trees. Certainly the tall, stately tulip-tree is abundant. But so are sugar maple, yellow buckeye, basswood, beech, yellow birch, northern red oak, and black cherry. In the Smokies and along the southern end of the Parkway, the Carolina silverbell appears as a major component of the cove hardwoods. In addition, a host of less common species grow in the narrow, secluded valleys.

20. The tall, straight trunks of tuliptrees are a common sight in the cove forests of lower elevations.

Areas with the greatest rainfall produce the best cove forests; as a result, the Virginia Blue Ridge examples are less diverse than their North Carolina counterparts. Still, the area surrounding the James River Visitor Center (M.P. 63.6) has a good variety (dominated by tuliptrees). The richest cove forests along the Parkway, however, occur nearest the Smokies. The best are found across from the Standing Rock Overlook (M.P. 441.4) and near Big Witch Tunnel (M.P. 461.2).

Where coves narrow into deeply cut stream bottoms and ravines, hemlocks constitute a greater part of the forest. Beneath them, tall thickets of rosebay rhododendron thrive. In some spots the effect of all this dark green foliage is nearly cavelike, usually complete with the gurgling and splashing of unseen water. Hemlock-dominated cove forests are rare along the Parkway, but one impressive example is found along the Trout Lake Trail at Moses Cone Park (M.P. 294.1), and another is visible from the roadway a short distance south of Mabry Mill (at M.P. 179.3).

Where the road crosses the French Broad River (M.P. 393.5), there exists a tree community not found anywhere else along the Parkway's entire length. The presence of basswoods and tuliptrees here demonstrates that this forest is related to the cove hardwoods, but also growing along the riverbanks are sycamores, river birches, box elder, and catalpa trees. More properly this community is classed as a *flood plain* forest, a type more common in the Carolina lowlands.

At the other end of the moisture spectrum from cove hardwoods, the oak-chestnut forest grades into a mixture of oaks and pines. This occurs in the driest mountain environments. Walk through an *oak-pine* woods, and you will find thin, sandy soil that produces not only stunted trees but a very limited number of wildflowers and other low plants. A few members of the drought-resistant heath family grow here (notably blueberries and mountain laurel), but they have little company.

Many such forests occur in the Asheville area (where less rain falls than elsewhere along the Parkway), and a number of ridgetops and low summits in both Virginia and North Carolina are covered with oaks and pines. Areas recently logged or farmed also support this forest type (an example occurs at M.P. 64.1, just south of the James River). Among oaks, the scarlet, black, and chestnut varieties are best suited to dry environments, and all of the southern Appalachian pines will live there: white pine, shortleaf pine, pitch pine, Virginia pine, and Table Mountain pine.

Those who recall that flowering plants have a more efficient water-conducting system than conifers may be surprised to find pines most common in dry areas. It is true that, given an adequate supply of water, flowering trees will use it more effectively than pines and their relatives. Where moisture is in short supply, though, pines have an advantage: they transport water less efficiently, but their small, waxy leaves conserve it better.

Despite their tolerance for dry conditions, pines (except the white pine) have no tolerance for shade. Often this works to their disadvantage. In barren areas where sunshine falls everywhere, they invade very successfully. Once their companion oaks grow large, however, young pines cannot survive beneath them. As a result, most oak-pine forests eventually become oak forests. Only the driest, most hostile sites in the southern Appalachians prevent oaks from dominating and remain clothed in pines.

Forests of Higher Elevations

In the Black Mountains, in the neighboring Craggies, and for much of the distance between Mount Pisgah (M.P. 408.6) and Great Smoky Mountains National Park, the Parkway traverses ridges and summits that approach or exceed 5,000 feet in elevation. The visitor who stops at a place like Buckeye Gap (M.P. 425.5) and investigates trees there may at first glance conclude that the cove hardwoods have spread up the slopes and taken over the moist high elevations. Many familiar cove trees are here: yellow buckeye, American beech, sugar maple, yellow birch. But many are missing, including the tuliptree and Carolina silverbell, which play major roles in the lower-elevation cove forest. More significantly, the proportions are different: in the cove hardwoods, dominance is shared by as many as eight or ten species of trees; at high elevations, only a few. At Buckeye Gap, for instance, two out of every three trees are beech.

This *northern hardwoods* forest may look familiar to visitors from the northeastern United States, for many trees found at these high elevations are common in the woods of Pennsylvania, New York, and New England. Joining them here in the southern Appalachians are a great number of shrubs and wildflowers, making the northern hardwoods forest nearly as diverse (in total kinds of plants) as the cove hardwoods. Many of the understory flora are also "Yankees," while some of the species present are limited to the southern mountains, and others are more generally distributed.

Different trees dominate northern hardwood forests at different sites. Yellow buckeye prevails in the wettest spots, while beech prefers drier conditions. In areas where rockslides have occurred, yellow birch takes over, thanks to its unique ability to germinate and grow on the tops of mossy boulders. A good illustration of this occurs near Steestachee Bald (at M.P. 437.6).

Another form of northern hardwoods forest is the *oak orchard,* where northern red oak holds sway as the most common tree. "Orchards" are found where the weather is harsh enough to stunt and prune the trees. This condition, coupled with a lack of shrubs in the understory, makes these forests resemble fruit orchards and is responsible for their name. The best examples are found on Apple Orchard Mountain (M.P. 76.5) and near Mount Pisgah at Frying Pan Gap (M.P. 409.6)

If the northern hardwoods forest along the Blue Ridge Parkway calls to mind the woods of New England, the *spruce-fir* zone of the highest summits is like a little piece of Canada. Above an elevation of 5,500 feet, northern weather has nurtured a northern forest.

There are two main tree species found here: the red spruce and the Fraser fir (the latter is found only in the southern Appalachians). Mountain ash, yellow birch, and fire or pin cherry appear in areas recently burned or logged, but in general, the summits belong to the evergreens. As you climb in elevation, spruce appears in the woods first, some trees growing as low as the 4,500-foot level on north-facing slopes. Firs generally enter the forest at an elevation of about 5,500 feet. On Mount Mitchell (M.P. 355.3), Richland Balsam (M.P. 431.4), and Waterrock Knob (M.P. 451.2), and along the Parkway in the vicinity of Devil's Courthouse (M.P. 422.4), these two trees crown some of the highest elevations of the southern Appalachians.

Like the spruces and firs found in Canada, both of these Appalachian evergreens are well suited to life in a harsh and stressful environment. During mountain winters, they stand up well under the weight of deep snow, and they resist frost damage better than broadleaf trees because fatty substances in the needles lower their freezing point. The two trees may be distinguished by several different features. Red spruce (known also as "he-balsam" in the mountains) has sharply pointed, four-sided needles; produces cones that hang downward; and may grow to a height of over 100 feet on favorable sites. Fraser fir (or "she-balsam"), on the other hand, seldom grows taller than 75 feet; it has flat, blunt needles and cones that point upward.

Another way to tell these two trees apart has emerged in recent years. The firs, unhappily, are the trees that have been turning rust-red, dropping their needles, and dying. (The phenomenon is especially visible in the spruce-fir forests south of Mount Pisgah, M.P. 408.6.) These trees are the victims of a European insect pest known as the balsam woolly aphid. Like the chestnut blight, the balsam woolly aphid (named for the stringy white secretions on its back) was accidentally imported into this country around 1900. For many years it damaged stands of balsam fir in the northern states and Canada; then, in the mid-1950s, infested Fraser firs were discovered on Mount Mitchell. Since that time, despite efforts to control it, the insect has spread to nearly every stand of Fraser fir in the southern Appalachians.

Because it has no effective natural defense against the balsam woolly aphid, the fir has fared badly. The aphid is a small sucking insect so tiny that individuals are difficult to find. It attacks the tree's bark and feeds on the juices of living tissues underneath. As it does so, the aphid injects poisonous saliva into the wood. The presence of a few insects has little effect on a Fraser fir, but once the aphids have multiplied into great masses, the tree's days are numbered. A heavy infestation can kill a fir in two years.

There have been no breakthroughs in the control of the balsam woolly aphid. It has no significant natural enemies in North America, and none of the half-dozen insect predators imported from Europe has had much effect on aphid populations. Certain insecticides kill them, but only when sprayed from the ground, which would necessitate a tree-by-tree offensive of overwhelming magnitude and expense. Christmas tree farms growing Fraser fir may be treated, but in the wild the insect pest will—at least for the present—remain unmolested by man.

21. Dead fir trees are common on Mount Mitchell, where the balsam woolly aphid first infested southern Appalachian trees.

Can the Fraser fir escape the virtual extinction that befell the American chestnut? Some researchers express a guarded optimism. The aphids tend to attack mature trees, bypassing most younger ones. As a result, healthy young seedlings grow up thickly among the skeletons of their parents in many stands. In addition, a few individual Fraser fir specimens seem to be showing signs of genetic resistance to balsam woolly aphid attack. "Some of those older trees are surviving," says Dr. Garrett Smathers, a professor at Western Carolina University. "They are giving us a gene pool, and by biological evolution the species may survive." Cautiously, he adds that "many colleagues don't share my opinion."[1] Visitors along the Blue Ridge Parkway through the coming decades will be able to witness the outcome of the Fraser fir's struggle for survival.

One other group of plant communities covers significant expanses of the high mountains. These areas are the *grass and heath balds,* found on a number of southern Appalachian summits and seen most prominently along the Parkway in the Craggy Gardens area (M.P. 364.6) and on Old Bald (M.P. 434.2). Though we may think of the balds as a forest type, there are no trees here to speak of. The grassy balds support grasses, sedges, and an assortment of other low-growing plants; the heath balds (also called "slicks") are covered by a collection of shrubs, predominantly rhododendron and mountain laurel. In places like Craggy Gardens, the two types of balds intergrade.

An observer, remembering other parallels between the mountain summits and northern latitudes, might conclude that the balds represent tundra vegetation, that they are miniature replicas of the vast treeless expanses above the Arctic Circle. But the balds are not tundra. They occur below treeline, on summits lower than many capped by spruce-fir forest. According to solid biological principles, there should be trees where the balds are found. Why aren't there? The question has spawned decades of speculative debate, but a definitive answer has yet to be found.

An early suggestion was that balds were caused by fires. It is true that a severe forest fire can completely eliminate trees from a ridge or

1. "Balsams May Survive Aphids," Waynesville, N.C., *Mountaineer* (May 4, 1979).

mountaintop; in a year or so, grasses and wildflowers take over the burn area, and in many ways the vegetation resembles that of a grassy bald. However, as subsequent years pass, shrubs and small trees spring up from seeds carried there by wind, water, and animals. Soon they grow to large sizes, crowding out many of the pioneering plants, and eventually the burn area returns to a forested state. In a century or two, the effects of the fire may be completely erased. Explaining why balds exist on certain southern Appalachian summits, therefore, involves two questions: we must figure out not only what formed balds initially but how they have been maintained.

One problem is that no one knows for sure how long balds have existed in the southern Appalachians. Some people claim that they are nothing more than the remains of mountaintop pastures cleared by the region's earliest settlers. But Elisha Mitchell (for whom Mount Mitchell was named) described the top of one peak in 1835 as "a vast meadow, without a tree to obstruct the prospect,"[2] an observation made during the infancy of the area's settlement. In addition, balds appear in Cherokee legends. Whether they are part of an ancient tradition, though, or were added in the last 200 years is arguable.

Interviews with old inhabitants seem to verify that at least some balds were indeed created by the area's European settlers. For the many whose origins cannot be explained this way, a number of other theories have been offered. One student of the problem suggests that ice and windstorms eliminated trees from certain summits. Another points to tree-killing insects as the culprits. Still others believe that the Cherokees and their ancestors originally burned off the forest to improve conditions for game and wild berries. Several well-known researchers maintain that climatic changes during the last few thousand years eliminated spruce and fir from some peaks, which later were taken over by the vegetation found on the balds today. Evidence can be found to support all of these hypotheses, and evidence can also be found to refute them all. Research may eventually show that different balds had different origins.

Once the trees were gone from the mountaintops, for whatever reason, something had to keep them from growing back. Some research sug-

2. Elisha Mitchell, "Notice of the Height of Mountains in North Carolina," *American Journal Science Arts* 35 (1835): 378.

gests that the thick grass prevented other plants from getting a foothold. Another suggestion is that harsh weather conditions prevent trees from recolonizing the balds. More recent studies conclude that the trampling and feeding of grazing animals inhibited the forest's return. It is a fact that sheep and cattle were pastured on balds for many years by mountain people, who could then use the lower, flatter lands for other agricultural purposes. Before the arrival of settlers, researchers think, native animals like deer and elk could have accomplished the same task.

Despite their many disagreements, scientists concur on one point: the balds are currently disappearing. Photographs taken in 1915 at Craggy Gardens (M.P. 364.6) compared with pictures taken today show that the area covered by grass and rhododendron has been rapidly shrinking. Other balds in the southern Appalachians are being swallowed by forest, as well. The trend seems to have begun when livestock grazing on the mountain summits ended. Unless man interferes with the natural process of succession, most balds—including the one at Craggy Gardens and most of those in the Smokies—will vanish during the next century.

Legacies of the Past

Unresolved questions about the origins of southern Appalachian balds, like geological disagreements about how the mountains were formed, illustrate a common point: it is a lot easier to understand how things are than to figure out how they got that way. To answer questions about events that occurred long before anyone was around to record them often takes a tremendous amount of scientific detective work.

Elements of another such detective story can be found along almost the entire length of the Parkway. It has already been pointed out that at higher elevations communities of plants exist that are normally associated with New England and Canada. Why do these northern plants thrive in southern mountains? They do so because the weather suits them; the cold winters and cool summers of the upper elevations are much like those of the region these plants commonly inhabit. That makes sense. But there is a second question that is harder to answer: how did they get here in the first place?

To explain the arrival of the northern red oak—whose range extends the length of the Appalachian chain, all the way up into Nova Scotia—

might not be very difficult. Conceivably, the species slowly covered distance under "squirrel power" as every year its acorns were buried a few hundred feet farther from its starting point.

But the distribution of some other southern Appalachian trees is not so easy to understand. In an isolated spot at Craggy Gardens (M.P. 364.6) grows a handful of large-toothed aspen, a species well known from Minnesota to Maine. Along the Fodderstack Trail at Doughton Park (M.P. 241.1) is another stand, of perhaps 50 specimens. The next place to the north where they are known to occur is in the vicinity of Roanoke, nearly 100 miles away.

Another species common in the northern United States and Canada is the white or paper birch. Several grow inconspicuously in the woods of Mount Mitchell (M.P. 355.3), and a few isolated stands exist elsewhere in the North Carolina mountains. Otherwise, the nearest paper birches grow in Rockbridge County, Virginia – a distance of over 200 miles as the seed flies.

Twelve more tree species, as well as other plants, exhibit similar patterns of distribution, occurring commonly across the northern states but only in isolated patches in the southern Appalachians. The fact that many kinds of animals follow the same trend is perhaps to be expected: mammals sometimes travel great distances, and birds and insects can populate far-off localities easily enough by flying to them. But what a surprise it must have been for early botanists to discover New England's red spruce on summits of the Blue Ridge and its neighboring ranges. The experience must have been the rough equivalent of Columbus coming ashore in the New World to find that its inhabitants spoke Italian.

It seemed reasonable to suppose that the Ice Ages of the past several million years were responsible for the current distributions of many plants and animals. During that period, the suggestion was, the species we now consider "northern" grew throughout southeastern North America. Glacial ice did not reach the area, but a cool climate did. Then, scientists theorized, as the weather warmed, many of the plants and animals followed the cold, not only pursuing the retreating glaciers but migrating slowly into the cooler high elevations as well. Eventually, trees like spruce, paper birch, and large-toothed aspen became separated into two populations by an intervening warm climate.

This hypothesis made sense, but the evidence needed to substantiate it has been found only during the last 50, and particularly the last 20, years. Perhaps the most obvious is the skeletal remains of animals that were discovered in caves in the southern Appalachian region. Deposits that were laid down in glacial times include bones from many mammals (and some birds) that today occur only in the coldest parts of Canada. The remains of a wolverine, for instance, were found in western Maryland.

Other evidence was discovered in mud scooped up from the bottoms of southern lakes. Sifting through sediments over 10,000 years old, researchers found pollen grains that could be identified under the microscope as those of currently northern plants. Spruce pollen was discovered as far south as Georgia and central Florida. As techniques have improved, scientists have been able to date pollen finds accurately and to reconstruct a picture of what these Ice Age forests were like. As a result, it now seems indisputable that the warming trend since glacial times has brought great changes to the southern Appalachians, and that the high-elevation forests found in the mountains today are remnants of an ancient past.

The Forest through the Seasons

Though the local schoolchildren may visit the Parkway in the spring to observe the leafing out of the forest, by the time most visitors arrive it is summer. The leaves have fully emerged and are engaged in making food whenever light is available. The food goes many places: into the trunk and limbs, expanding their size; into storage, to be held through the winter and used in the first rush of growth next spring; into the production of seeds; into the digestive systems of countless animals.

Parkway visitors find that in addition to the miles of forest that line the roadsides, some spots merit special attention. Along the Smart View Trail (M.P. 154.5) there are impressive oaks three and four feet in diameter. Moses Cone Park (M.P. 294) has perhaps a greater number of tree species than any other Parkway locality (some were planted by the Cone family). The Linville Falls area (M.P. 316.4) boasts huge Carolina hemlocks.

As summer begins to fade into the shorter days and chillier nights of autumn, broadleaf trees start to change, coloring first in cooler higher

22. Tall hemlocks form a large part of the forest canopy at Linville Falls.

elevations. Leaves essential to the tree through the warm months will become liabilities when the frosts and snows of winter come, so they must be jettisoned. First a tree cuts off its leaves' supply of nutrients. Without the minerals that were provided all summer through the efforts of the roots, the leaves can no longer manufacture chlorophyll. Gradually they use up what chlorophyll they have, and their green color fades. Other pigments, present before but masked by chlorophyll, now appear. Where the sun shines brightest, the yellows and oranges of autumn develop fastest. South-facing slopes, the south sides of trees, and the outermost leaves turn color first. Some have likened the onset of fall colors to the performance of a symphony; if so, the weather is its composer. Cool nights initiate the music, signaling the trees that winter is approaching. Sunshine intensifies the colors, especially the reds. Rain, on the other hand, rinses them away. Strong winds may blow leaves off before their colors have faded. A hard frost or an early snow will bring the symphony to an abrupt end—turning leaves, like garden plants, a lifeless brown. Every year the score is arranged differently.

Autumn is the season when southern Appalachian trees attract the most attention. Thousands of visitors flock to the Blue Ridge Parkway at this time, making October far and away the busiest month of the year. Sections of the road near special points of interest (like Mabry Mill, M.P. 176.1) may have bumper-to-bumper traffic on peak weekends.

October passes, and by the first of November most of the leaves are gone. Visitors depart, the first snows fall, and the trees slip into dormancy. Even pines, hemlocks, firs, and spruces slow down. Though they have kept their leaves, there will be no water available to them during the frigid days ahead. Animal life, dependent as it is on trees, must make dramatic adjustments to survive the winter essentially without them. Many animals also become dormant. Some leave the area for other climates. Those that stay cannot depend on leaves for food; instead, they subsist on seeds, berries, buds, the inner bark of twigs and branches— and each other. People tend to think that cold weather is what stresses animals in winter. Not so—it is the lack of food that brings them hardship.

But the winter finally wanes, as well. The first warm sunshine in February strikes the bare trunks of the broadleaf trees, and the sap begins to flow. (Again, as maple sugarers can attest, things happen first on the south side of the tree.) Buds swell. With the onset of even warmer

The erosion-resistant granite of Looking Glass Rock can be viewed from M.P. 417.1.

Like thousands of other southern Appalachian waterfalls, Fallingwater Cascades (M.P. 83.1) is nourished by the region's abundant rainfall.

Flame azalea adds a splash of color to a scene of New York ferns.

In years when spring arrives late in the mountains, visitors can enjoy blooming dogwoods before the pink of the redbuds has faded.

Large-flowered trillium, a member of the lily family, brightens the woods in May.

Catawba or purple rhododendron at Craggy Gardens (M.P. 364.4) produces what is perhaps the Parkway's most spectacular floral display.

A skipper butterfly enjoys a meal of milkweed nectar.

The wood frog, found all along the Parkway except at the highest elevations, is one of the first amphibians to emerge from hibernation in the spring.

Sticky round toe pads enable the gray treefrog to climb with ease.

An encounter with this red eft (eastern newt) enlivened a hike along the Fodderstack Trail at Doughton Park (M.P. 241.1).

Well-guarded by its mother, a black bear cub scrambles up a nearby tree trunk at the first sign of danger.

Raccoons generally spend the daylight hours in trees, but come to earth at night to forage.

23. In some spots along the Parkway, today's fall colors have been enhanced by yesterday's human labors. In this 1939 scene, workmen move a maple from the deep woods to the roadside.

weather, the procession of woodland wildflowers bursts forth as they race to live their lives while there is still sunlight on the forest floor. Then May arrives, schoolchildren make their first field trips to the woods, and the story of trees begins all over again.

Insects and Other Invertebrates

Once, while giving a campfire talk, I referred to mosquitoes as "wildlife" and got a good laugh. The word "wildlife" inspires images of deer bounding gracefully up roadside embankments, inquisitive raccoons prowling through campgrounds, and hawks soaring high over southern Appalachian ridges—not of mosquitoes whining around one's ears in the middle of the night. My comment, however, had not been intended as a joke. As native animals of southern mountains, insects and other invertebrates rate as wildlife, too.

Furthermore, I've always considered them the "visible wildlife." Deer, bear, bobcats, foxes, and most other popular wild animals are very adept at avoiding humans, and as a result few people see them. Many visitors bemoan the fact that they have traveled for miles on the Parkway and haven't encountered any wildlife.

Yet they need only look around them. In the trees, on flowers, beneath dead leaves on the forest floor, in grassy pastures and fields, in ponds and streams, both day and night and through every season of the year, the insects and their relatives pervade the southern mountains. Their numbers dwarf all other forms of wildlife combined. Only about 100 kinds of mammals are found in the southern Appalachians, and perhaps 300 varieties of birds. In the same area, biologists have discovered 600 species of ground beetles alone. Include with these the timber beetles, flower beetles, carrion beetles, fungus beetles, leaf beetles, flea beetles, weevils, and all the other beetle families; then add bees, wasps, flies, ants, butterflies, grasshoppers, crickets, true bugs, worms, centipedes, millipedes, spiders, ticks, protozoans, snails, crayfish, and all the remaining invertebrate groups and one begins to grasp the immensity of their numbers. Well over 90 percent of all visible living things in the southern Appalachians are invertebrates.

Nonetheless, the Parkway's invertebrates are generally overlooked. Are they less appealing, less attractive than other wildlife? Some might argue that they are. (Admittedly, invertebrates are rarely the models for stuffed animals or picture postcards.) Are they less interesting than other wildlife? Hardly. Invertebrates are every bit as colorful and diverse as

Tom R. Johnson

better-known Blue Ridge animals. Just one example: bats command the attention of both biologists and laymen because of their marvelous radar-like system of echolocation, which enables them to pinpoint and catch flying insects in complete darkness. Less publicized but no less amazing is the fact that certain moths have evolved a "radar-detection" ability: they are able to intercept the signals of an oncoming bat and take evasive action to avoid becoming its meal. Other examples of invertebrates with special traits and adaptations are legion. With all its diversity and inter-action between organisms, the world of invertebrates is like a miniature of the world of larger wildlife. Best of all, it can be found as near as the edge of the parking lot, and observed with equipment no more special than the human eye.

What are invertebrates? To put it simply, they include every form of animal life that does not have a backbone. Fish, amphibians, reptiles, birds, and mammals—all of which do have backbones—are grouped as vertebrates; they are the subjects of other chapters. All other kinds of animal found along the Blue Ridge Parkway are invertebrates.

The largest group among the invertebrates is the insects. It would be impossible here even to begin describing all the varieties that can be found along the entire Parkway, for as one group of authors has noted, "over a thousand kinds may occur in a fair-sized backyard."[1] It is easy enough, however, to separate them from other invertebrates: any small creature with six legs and a body divided into three parts (head, thorax, and abdomen) is an insect.

The remaining invertebrates include a wide array of organisms. Many of them – called protozoans, rotifers, nematodes, and other unfamiliar names – will be encountered only by visitors with microscopes. Others are much more obvious: earthworms, snails, millipedes, centipedes, mites, and spiders are all among the more readily recognizable southern Appalachian invertebrates.

Where to Find Insects and Their Relatives

Roll over a rotting log on the forest floor and look underneath. In one motion you have opened the door to (or rather, lifted the roof off) a whole community of southern Appalachian invertebrates.

Representatives of some groups are very common on the forest floor. Earthworms, for example, may occur in densities as thick as a half-million per acre in some woods. Their thousands of tunnels help air and water to penetrate the soil, cultivating the forest as surely as careful gardeners tend their tomatoes and corn. Tiny mites are also present in large numbers, different types feeding on different foods. Some eat decaying plant material, some concentrate on soil fungi, and some prey on other minute animals found in soil and leaf litter. Many of these victims – tiny roundworms, amoebae, and an assortment of related microorganisms – are too small to be seen by the unaided eye, but their immense numbers make a large contribution in the breakdown of dead plant and animal materials that cover the ground each year. The miniature predators

---

1. Donald J. Borror, Dwight M. De Long, and Charles A. Triplehorn, *An Introduction to the Study of Insects,* 4th ed. (New York: Holt, Rinehart, and Winston, 1976), 1.

among them do not directly participate in this process of decomposition, but play a role in keeping the forest floor community in balance.

Other invertebrates appear occasionally. Maybe you'll uncover a snail hiding out until darkness arrives, when it will crawl forth for a nighttime meal of leaves, mushrooms, and other plant materials. More than 150 varieties of snails populate the southern Appalachians. A number of kinds of spiders will also seek shelter under a dead log, and some find their prey there as well. Joining them may be harvestmen (or daddy-long-legs), which are close relatives. Many species of beetles, too, live in close association with the forest floor. The predatory ground beetles are especially common there, and the larvae of other beetle families (known to fishermen as "grubs") sometimes live beneath rotten wood or even in it.

You won't have to roll over very many logs before you run across your first millipede, or "thousand-legger." In fact, you may not have to disturb any logs at all, because millipedes are frequently encountered on trails along the Parkway, looking like armored caterpillars as they lumber methodically across the soil. Disturb one, and it will curl itself up into a protective spiral. There are about 500 types of millipedes in the southern mountains, many of them quite colorful. Conspicuous millipedes in the Peaks of Otter area (M.P. 85.9), for instance, include a five-inch dusty-blue and red variety, and a smaller yellow and black one. Like earthworms, millipedes are able to eat and digest dead leaves and other organic matter on the forest floor, and so play a big part in recycling the minerals and other nutrients they contain.

There may be a centipede under that log as well. Like the related millipedes, centipedes have more legs than most visitors would care to count; the difference is that centipedes have only one pair per body segment, while millipedes have two pairs. Rather than pick them up to check this trait (centipedes bite), identify them by their behavior. Invariably, a centipede suddenly exposed to light will run for cover. They are remarkably quick, a useful trait because the centipede (unlike the millipede) is a predator. Centipedes use their speed to capture other invertebrates.

The visitor with enough time and interest could make a whole study of the invertebrate communities that live under logs. He or she might even begin to notice certain trends: that heavily decayed logs support a group of organisms different from those under intact logs; that sowbugs,

24. Snails are most active at night and in wet weather. They emerge
from protection to feed on leaves, mushrooms, and other plant materials.

centipedes, and many other invertebrates live only where it is damp; that the presence of an ant colony frequently excludes most other animals (since many ants are predators). To those visitors who plan to investigate the dark world beneath a fallen log, a request: return it to darkness when you are finished by rolling the log back. Disturb the natural environment as little as possible.

The blooming of field wildflowers in July and August provides another fine opportunity to observe southern Appalachian invertebrates, especially insects. Many of the blossoms produce great quantities of nectar and attract a wide variety of potential pollinators. Butterfly weed, boneset, Joe-Pye weed, ironweed, and goldenrod all lure their share, but perhaps the best bug-watching can be done by pulling up a folding chair to a stand of common milkweed on a sunny July afternoon.

It takes no effort or initiative whatsoever to spot the visiting butterflies. If the flowers are fresh and the day pretty, they will be there in clouds, half a dozen on every plant, flitting from milkweed to milkweed, sipping nectar with their long tonguelike proboscises, and jostling one another like kids at a crowded dinner table. Probably the most common butterflies along the Blue Ridge Parkway are the swallowtails, named for the tabs or "tails" that extend from the back of their hindwings. The showiest one is the large tiger swallowtail. The majority of these are yellow with black striping, but many females have no yellow at all; as a result, they bear a great resemblance to the pipevine swallowtail, also found along the Parkway. Pipevine swallowtails are avoided by hungry birds because of their noxious taste, and the dark tiger swallowtails may gain protection from predators by being disguised as their unpalatable cousins.

The best known of the bad-tasting insects, and perhaps North America's most popular butterfly, is the monarch—also a milkweed visitor. The monarch butterfly's prominent orange and black pattern is a common sight around milkweed plants—and no wonder, for the adults not only feed on milkweed nectar but lay their eggs on the plant's leaves, and the larvae grow and develop eating milkweed. It is from the plant's juices that monarchs acquire the bitter taste that predators avoid. The bright colors of the adult serve as a warning to birds, most of which quickly

25. The monarch butterfly is one of many insects that visit milkweed blooms for a meal of nectar.

learn to avoid preying upon monarchs. An edible butterfly known as the viceroy (occasionally found along the Parkway) gains protection from predators by sporting a color pattern strikingly similar to that of the monarch. This deception is a form of what biologists call *mimicry*; in fact, it is perhaps the best-known and most frequently quoted example in nature.

Other butterflies join the abundant monarchs and swallowtails on milkweed blooms. Several small, quick-flying varieties called skippers dart from plant to plant. Large orange-brown butterflies, grandiosely named "great spangled fritillaries," are occasionally present, as well as pearl crescents and painted ladies.

Joining the butterflies are several of the very few day-flying moths. One, the Virginia ctenucha, can be identified by its black wings, bright orange head, and feathery antennae. Hawk moths, also nectar feeders, may startle you as they zip around and hover before milkweed blooms like hummingbirds. The more attention you pay to the invertebrate world, the more unusual creatures you are likely to encounter.

A closer look at the milkweed plant itself may reveal other, more permanent residents. One, of course, is the monarch butterfly caterpillar. It crawls about the plant, eating leaves, stems, and blossoms indiscriminately. Monarch larvae seem to be easier to find than other caterpillars; a careful search will almost always turn up one or more in a patch of milkweed plants. Like the adult monarch, the caterpillar is protected by its foul-tasting body fluids and signals its unpalatability with a bold black, white, and yellow color pattern. Perhaps with this security it need not be as inconspicuous as other caterpillars to survive. Joining it on the plant are milkweed bugs and the red milkweed beetle, insects that share the monarch butterfly's showy warning colors and, presumably, its unpleasant taste.

Crab spiders are other colorful invertebrates found on milkweed. Their attractive pinks, whites, and yellows are not meant to be conspicuous, however; they are camouflage. Crab spiders hide among milkweed flowers and seize unwary insects that land to feed there. Occasionally, orb weaver spiders make milkweed their base of operations. Some of these are large enough to tackle butterflies, and even monarchs are not spared their attention: spiders are one of the few predators that seem to be unaffected by the monarch's defenses.

26. Monarch butterfly caterpillars feed on the leaves of milkweed. Like
the adults, larvae are bad-tasting to predators and have bold coloration to
advertise that fact.

27. Milkweed bugs join monarch caterpillars in feeding on the milkweed plant.

28. Some orb weaver spiders are large enough to capture and subdue butterflies in their webs.

Another opportunity to experience the variety of invertebrate life comes in August, after darkness falls. Since the first warm days of spring, moths populated the forests at night, and visitors have seen them gathered around bright spotlights and well-lit windows. Wherever wet meadows occur (for instance, south of the Rocky Knob area, M.P. 169, and around Linville Falls, M.P. 316.4), fireflies have blinked by the hundreds through the early summer, and in August still flash occasionally. (Fireflies, by the way, are actually beetles.) But the most impressive display of insect activity is just beginning. It is one not to be seen but to be listened to.

The insect sounds of late summer nights are the products of various crickets and their relatives, the katydids. (Visitors sometimes identify them as treefrogs or cicadas, but this is erroneous. Most treefrogs do their singing in the spring, when they mate in woodland ponds; cicadas, large insects unrelated to crickets, generally produce their lazy, buzzing song on hot summer afternoons.) In lower elevations, the first insect sounds are heard during the last week of July. The chorus grows louder and spreads upward as days pass. By mid-August, nighttime in southern Appalachian deciduous forests is clamorous with insect noises.

To fully experience this natural symphony, walk a short distance up one of the Parkway's woodland trails after dark. Stop, turn off your flashlight, and listen. The loudest music is that produced by the katydids, a surging, pulsating chorus repeating their name: "katy-*did*, katy-*did*." A katydid is a clumsy green variation of a grasshopper, whose leaflike appearance helps it escape predators. Visitors sometimes encounter them during daylight hours, usually on tents, car roofs, or picnic tables in the early morning. Few connect them, however, with their serenade of the night before.

If the night is a warm one, you will hear throngs of these nocturnal musicians. Nonetheless, the careful listener will be able to pick out the performance of individual insects. As an aid, cup your hands and place them behind your ears; then by turning your head, you can zero in on specific sounds. Your first realization will be that the soloists are above you, in the forest canopy. It is there that katydids spend their lives, feeding on leaves and remaining camouflaged by their shape and color.

Your second discovery may be that there are other voices in the night, as well. Throughout the southern Appalachians, various crickets sing through the late summer, softly underscoring the louder katydids.

Many tree crickets emit long trills; most ground and field crickets chirp. Different kinds inhabit different areas, but a sharp listener in a good location may detect as many as half a dozen insect sounds.

The songs of crickets and katydids are mating calls. Insects that are active only at night must all cope with the same problem: how to locate one another in the darkness. Fireflies have developed a unique solution, utilizing visual signals. Female moths emit a scent that attracts the males. Crickets and katydids use sound, produced (usually by males only) by rubbing one wing against the other, in a rhythm that is distinct for each species.

The night music continues into early fall. Insects are significantly influenced by temperature, and cool nights reduce the orchestra's volume. (The snowy tree cricket is so sensitive to temperature that by counting the number of its chirps in a 15-second period and adding 40, you can arrive at a fairly accurate estimate of the temperature in degrees Fahrenheit.) The first hard frosts kill the crickets and katydids, silencing the music until the following year.

Autumn produces the last burst of invertebrate activity in the mountains. Many invertebrates seek protected cracks and crevices in which to hide during their winter dormancy. Some moth caterpillars spin cocoons to serve as cold weather shelters. On the forest floor, beetles, spiders, and other residents burrow deeper into the soil and leaf litter for protection from impending frosts. A number of invertebrates leave only eggs to carry the species into the next year.

A few insects, like the migratory birds, fly south. Monarch butterflies drift and flutter southward by the thousands, floating along and across the southern Appalachian ridges during the latter part of September. One of the best places to view their migration from the Parkway is at Cherry Cove Overlook (M.P. 415.7). Other butterflies are often seen in the monarchs' company, among them mourning cloaks, painted ladies, and red admirals.

Despite the chill stillness that winter brings with it, visitors willing to get their feet wet can still find active invertebrates, even in the depths of January and February. For no matter how cold the weather gets, the mountain streams never freeze solid, and patrolling their bottoms are a host of insects and insect relatives.

The best known of the stream's invertebrates are crayfish, which look like miniature lobsters. Different kinds live in different types of water-courses: some prefer a sandy bottom; others thrive in mud, gravel, or rocky areas. They eat a mixture of plant and animal foods. Like most stream residents, crayfish are hosts to many parasitic worms, which also rank as important aquatic invertebrates.

Insects are found in the winter streams as well. Almost without exception they are the larval forms of insects we see on land during the warmer months. Called "nymphs," they are to their adult stages what a caterpillar is to a butterfly. The nymphs are wingless and generally breathe by means of gills. A number of kinds are found in streams along the Parkway.

Mayfly nymphs are typical examples. The adult insects are flimsy creatures, with long tail filaments and two pairs of transparent wings that fold over their backs. Adult mayflies usually emerge from water in spring or early summer, sometimes appearing in great hordes. They live just long enough to mate and lay eggs, a period that may be only a matter of hours. The nymphs of many species, on the other hand, live in streams and ponds for up to three years, frequently hiding under rocks, logs, and other stream debris and feeding on tiny bits of organic matter.

Also present under winter ice are the larvae of stoneflies, crane flies, dobsonflies, certain dragonflies, caddisflies, and other insects. Most are easily located by checking their common hiding places. Caddisflies, how-ever, may escape the notice of all but knowledgeable observers. Many of these nymphs (the adults of which resemble small moths) build protec-tive cases around themselves, hollow cylinders no larger than cigarette butts. Some are made of tiny stones cemented together by the insect. Other species use twigs or bits of dead leaves as their construction mate-rials. Caddisfly cases camouflage their owners and, like a snail's shell, give them some measure of protection from their many predators. Other varieties of caddisfly larvae spin nets, which they use to strain food parti-cles from the flowing waters of the stream.

Invertebrates and the Mountains

Previous chapters have stressed how the plant life of the southern Appalachian region has been influenced by the mountains. In many cases the invertebrate group is intimately linked to plants (the close relation-

29. Stonefly nymphs remain active in mountain streams throughout the winter. They are an important trout food.

ship between the balsam woolly aphid and the Fraser fir of the highest southern Appalachian summits is one example), and it should come as no surprise that the mountains affect the invertebrates, as well. For instance, streams that flow through crystalline and metamorphic rock (as do most of the streams along the Parkway) tend to have soft water and fewer invertebrates than waters whose many dissolved minerals (hard water) support a richer animal population. Even the forest type that a creek passes through influences the variety of aquatic insects found there. This is because many of the stream's residents rely on dead leaves as their food supply, and leaves — even when dead — differ in many ways. The tough, waxy rhododendron leaves, for example, drift downstream almost untouched by aquatic invertebrates.

The great age of the southern Appalachians has enabled many groups of invertebrates, as well as plants, to evolve here without the cataclysmic interference of ice, oceans, or volcanoes. In the millions of years since these mountains were first formed, groups like the millipedes and scorpionflies have developed here and radiated outward all across North America. Further research (sorely needed in the area of invertebrates) will undoubtedly uncover many more instances of the mountains' special relationship with the insects and their kin.

The Roles of Invertebrates

At Linville Falls (M.P. 316.4) in North Carolina, people buttonhole park rangers. "What is wrong with the pine trees?" they ask. Around Roanoke, Virginia (M.P. 112.2), the pines are fine, but observant visitors spot other problems. "Why are the locust trees dying?" they inquire.

In both places, invertebrates have been at work. Generally unseen themselves, the damage they have done in the course of their feeding is what has caught the public eye.

The insect responsible for dead and dying white pines around Linville Falls is the introduced pine sawfly. An imported problem, like the balsam woolly aphid, this native of Europe first appeared in North America in 1914 on nursery trees in New Haven, Connecticut, and quickly took to its new American home, feeding voraciously on the needles of native pines. It became a serious destroyer of trees in many places, particularly in the Great Lakes states where its favorite white pines are common.

The introduced pine sawfly did not make its way to North Carolina until 1977, when it was discovered at Linville Falls. Here in the South it has become even more destructive, because the longer warm season allows the insect to produce two and three generations a year. Through the late spring, summer, and early fall, thousands of hungry sawfly larvae feast on the needles of white pines. The trees frequently die, victims either of the sawfly itself or of a fungus that easily invades sawfly-weakened trees. The introduced pine sawfly is slowly spreading its range through the southern mountains. Recently, however, great progress has been made in its control. Biologists have released thousands of tiny wasps, members of several species that parasitize the sawflies and kill large numbers. The white pines will be spared the fate of the Fraser fir.

In Virginia, the black locust trees have been attacked in recent years by a native insect called the locust leaf miner. The adult is a small beetle about the size of a ladybug; the damage, however, is done by its larvae. These tunnel about in the locust leaf, feeding on the plant material inside. Leaves attacked by the leaf miner larvae wither and turn brown, and large stands of locust can be sorry sights by late summer. The work of this insect is evident along much of the Virginia section of the Parkway. Fortunately, black locusts generally survive the attentions of the locust leaf miner, probably because their leaves are not seriously damaged until near the end of the growing season.

In the cases of the leaf miner, the introduced pine sawfly, and the balsam woolly aphid, observers encounter the significant effects of invertebrates without ever seeing the invertebrates themselves. Usually, however, the situation is reversed: we see the invertebrates but have no idea of the role they play in nature. "Why were these things ever created?" we fume, waving our hands through a cloud of exasperating gnats.

Every invertebrate, though, like every other plant and animal, forms a strand in the complex web of nature. Because the world of insects and their relatives is so diverse, it is not startling to find that many have unique roles. Yucca moths are the sole pollinators of yucca plants. (A species of yucca native to the Atlantic coast grows near human habitation along the Parkway.) Ladyslippers depend upon just a few varieties of bees for their continued existence. The importance of insects in pollinating the world's flowering plants is inestimable.

The role of most invertebrates, however, is to eat and be eaten. The thousands of insect species that feed on plant matter in turn become the food of other members of the animal kingdom. Under a log, the snail is eaten by a ground beetle, which later becomes the meal of a toad. On a milkweed flower, the crab spider which has captured a nectar-seeking fly is soon found by a song sparrow and fed to the bird's young. In the dark of an August evening, a shrew stumbles across a tree cricket and quickly swallows it. Below the surface of a mountain stream, a trout eats a stonefly larva.

There is no end to the number of food chains that involve invertebrates. Nearly all the other animals living in the southern Appalachians are affected by them in one way or another. Indeed, even humans are drawn into this complex web, generally by serving as a source of food for mountain insects. The gnats, "no-see-ums," and infrequent Parkway mosquitoes that pester us all help support other forms of life: spiders, dragonflies, flycatchers, and swallows are just a few.

So if invertebrate representatives of the Blue Ridge Parkway wildlife bite you during your visit here, perhaps you will find some solace in the knowledge that you have made a contribution to the natural systems of the southern Appalachian mountains.

Fish, Amphibians, and Reptiles

No one who has lazed away an afternoon fishing, splashed after frogs as a child, or worried about snakebite needs an introduction to the subjects of this chapter. Fish, amphibians, and reptiles are familiar in some measure to everyone. Handbooks on them are readily available, and many visitors to the Blue Ridge Parkway rate as experts – they are avid fishermen, for instance, or amateur herpetologists (students of frogs, salamanders, snakes, lizards, and their kin). The southern Appalachians have impressed their own stamp on these animal groups, though, and it is the special qualities of the mountain fish, amphibians, and reptiles that are highlighted here.

Fish

A mountaintop park does not seem a likely place to find fish: reason suggests that most rain falling there will rapidly drain downhill, leaving no bodies of water large enough to support fish. Indeed, much of the Blue Ridge Parkway does wind along the crests of the southern Appalachian ridges, where the small, spring-fed mountain streams arise on either side of the road and flow away from it. At lower elevations, however, the Parkway traverses hollows and coves, and crosses river valleys that divide the range. Here water is plentiful and fish common. And even a high-altitude mountain brook small enough to jump across will likely be populated by darters, dace, or colorful brook trout.

In addition, humans have created homes for fish in the southern Appalachians where nature did not. Along the Blue Ridge Parkway, there are 13 artificial lakes and ponds, ranging in size from pools no larger than a city lot to 47-acre Price Lake (M.P. 296.7). Some were constructed by the National Park Service to enhance recreation along the Parkway; others had already been established before the road was built.

To the delight of anglers, almost all of them contain fish. Rainbow, brook, and brown trout – popular cold-water game fish – swim in many lakes and ponds. One or more of these species can be found in Otter Lake (M.P. 63.1), Abbot Lake (M.P. 86), Trout and Little Trout Lakes

Tom R. Johnson

(M.P. 294), Sims Pond (M.P. 295.9), and Price Lake. In addition, warmer waters contain bass and bream (the local name for several kinds of sunfish). Otter Lake, Bass Lake (M.P. 294), and Price Lake are the best spots for these.

Many of the fish found in the Parkway's lakes and ponds are imports: like some plants and animals mentioned elsewhere in this book, they were introduced here by humans. Some were purposely stocked in local waters: rainbow trout, for instance, are native to the mountains of the American West, and brown trout were brought over from Europe. Others showed up in Parkway waters by accident – mixed in with hatchery trout, perhaps, or dumped in as a fisherman's unused bait. Examples include golden shiners (present in some of the larger lakes) and carp (found in Otter Lake).

In four places the Blue Ridge Parkway crosses sizable streams or rivers: the James River (M.P. 63.7), the Roanoke River (M.P. 114.8), the Linville River (M.P. 316.6), and the French Broad River (M.P. 393.5). All support a large diversity of fish. Like those in Parkway lakes and ponds, some are native and others introduced.

From a naturalist's standpoint, however, the Parkway has waters more interesting than man-made lakes or man-influenced rivers: its streams.

Despite the road's generally high elevation, there are over 75 miles of mountain brook flowing within the National Park Service boundaries. Some watercourses have been stocked with rainbow and brown trout, but for the most part these waters are essentially wild and little affected by people. Good examples are the upper stretches of Rock Castle Creek near Rocky Knob (M.P. 169) and Basin and Cove Creeks at Doughton Park (M.P. 241.1). These and other remote southern Appalachian streams contain only one fish that significantly interests anglers—the brook trout, a mountain native. A striking olive-colored fish with bright red, blue, and white markings, the brook trout can be found wherever water is clean and cold. Streams with holes no more than knee-deep may support populations of "brookies."

The high mountain streams hold many other fish that sportsmen rarely pay any attention to. They have evocative names: fantail darters, hornyhead chubs, stonerollers, and several dozen more. All are relatively small and are generally referred to collectively as "minnows" by people not familiar with them. Lurking near the bottom or hiding beside logs and stones, the southern Appalachian darters, dace, chubs, and their relatives form important links in aquatic food chains, feeding on tiny stream invertebrates and being eaten in turn by trout.

Though we tend to think of streams as separate from the forest, fish —large and small—are involved in the fabric of life in the woods as well. The trout at the end of the creek's food chain may suddenly become an intermediate link in the forest when flipped onto the bank by a dexterous raccoon or speared by a hungry green heron. In addition, by preying upon aquatic insect larvae, fish influence the numbers of adult insects that eventually emerge into the air. (Longnose dace, for instance, feed heavily on the larvae of blackflies.) Fish, in other words, are full members of the southern Appalachian natural community.

The mountains influence fish populations in several ways. Most obviously, the high elevations produce cold water, a prerequisite for many species. Brook trout are perhaps the most temperature-sensitive of native mountain fish; they cannot survive in streams warmer than 75°F (which for humans is still a pretty cool swim). As a result, several southern Appalachian fish, including the brook trout, are not present in the South outside the mountains but are common and widely distributed in the waters of the northern United States and Canada.

30. Brook trout live in the highest elevations, sometimes occurring in streams that do not support any other kinds of fish.

In addition, the factors that determine a stream's invertebrate population have an indirect effect on its fish. Recall that local rock types and the surrounding forest make a difference to aquatic insects and their relatives. The fish are influenced in turn: streams with a large variety of invertebrate life, for instance, often support a greater diversity of fish.

The mountains have also had a significant impact on the evolution of southern Appalachian fish. Because waters that flow to the Atlantic Ocean are divided by the crest of the mountains from those that drain into the Gulf of Mexico, the fish that live in these waters are separated, as well. If a trout in the Linville River (M.P. 316.6) wanted to reach the nearby waters of Brushy Creek (near M.P. 317.7), it would have to swim downstream all the way to Charleston, South Carolina; through the Atlantic and the Gulf of Mexico; then up the Mississippi, Tennessee, and Toe rivers to reach its destination—an improbable journey of thousands of miles, although we can walk the straight-line overland distance in 20 minutes. This separation of watersheds has existed for millions of years, time enough for fish on either side of the divide to evolve and develop into different varieties and strains. The mountains, therefore, have helped create a greater diversity of fish than occurs in any flatland of similar area.

Under the circumstances, visitors might be surprised to find some kinds of fish on both sides of the divide. Again, geologic forces are responsible. Since fast-eroding Atlantic-bound streams have in past centuries broken through the ridge crest and pirated westward-flowing waters, they have captured some western fish as well. Examples of this mixing of fish species occur in most Blue Ridge waters.

Amphibians

It was dark and pouring rain, and I was driving along the Parkway in second gear, watching the pavement lines go past one by one. Fortunately, the stretch of road that swings around Roanoke is relatively flat and straight, and on a weeknight in March there was no traffic whatsoever. I noticed a lot of small sticks on the pavement but paid them no special attention until I began to perceive that some of them were moving. The next time one appeared in the headlights, I stopped the car and ran out through the puddles to investigate.

The "sticks" turned out to be spotted salamanders, eight-inch-long creatures whose slippery black skin is decorated with round yellow spots. Salamanders are known as "spring lizards" to many mountain residents; however, salamanders are amphibians (along with frogs and toads), while lizards are reptiles. The two groups can be differentiated by the fact that the amphibians have smooth skin rather than dry scales like reptiles, and lizards have claws but salamanders do not. These spotted salamanders, cued by the first warm rain of spring, were on their way to local ponds to lay their eggs.

Rain is probably the primary factor responsible for making the southern Appalachians one of the foremost havens for amphibians in North America. Amphibians are inseparably tied to moisture. Many kinds spend their entire lives in water, and the rest either return there to lay their eggs or rely on dampness to keep themselves from dehydrating and dying. And the southern Appalachian region, as has already been mentioned, is a very wet place. It can also be cool at high mountain elevations, and frogs, toads, and salamanders are generally very tolerant of cold – another reason for their abundance here.

Having identified the spotted salamander there in the middle of the Parkway, I let it proceed on its way while I – not so tolerant of wet and cold – got back in the car.

There are 34 kinds of salamanders living in the southern Appalachians, and at least two-thirds of these can be found somewhere along the Blue Ridge Parkway. Despite the fact that these figures seem small when compared with the many varieties of insects, birds, or mammals that occur here, in total numbers salamanders rate as plentiful indeed: as a group they are the most common vertebrate animals in the southern mountains.

Visitors rarely get a sense of their abundance; occasions when they can be found all over the roadway are rare. And salamanders, like many other Blue Ridge animals, are active almost exclusively at night. For a person armed with a flashlight, however, they are not difficult to observe if you know where to look.

The surest place to find salamanders is near a mountain stream. Walk along one of the Parkway's many creekside trails shortly after dark; shine your light along the banks and on rocks and logs. With perseverance, you will eventually spot a seal salamander, or perhaps one of the dusky salamanders. These dark-colored species live in the water, or very near it, and emerge at night to hunt for prey. Salamanders (in fact, amphibians in general) have very broad-minded tastes in food: if it's small and it moves, a salamander will eat it. Practically speaking, this means that salamanders feed mostly on insects, slugs, worms, and other invertebrates.

Larger predators, in turn, are equally indiscriminate when it comes to eating salamanders; any meat-eating animal that can catch them will do so. Raccoons, bears, skunks, snakes, and opossums all take salamanders at times; larger fish in the streams will also eat them. For the most part, salamanders must rely on their wriggling quickness and slippery skin to escape enemies. A couple of types do possess other defenses: the eastern newt, for instance, has enough poisonous glands in its skin to frustrate predators, and the slimy salamander releases a sticky mucus that often discourages animals (and people) who handle it.

During daylight hours, the more aquatic salamanders hide either under wet rocks and logs or in burrows along stream banks. They can sometimes be uncovered in these places, but the visitor who plans to search for salamanders during the day may be more successful pursuing terrestrial kinds. Many southern Appalachian salamanders do not spend any of their lifetime in water. Rather, they hatch fully developed from eggs laid in damp places under forest debris, and live their lives in the forest.

Carefully roll over a log or lift up its dead bark. Dark, moist places like these frequently conceal salamanders. Some, like the three- to four-inch-long redback salamander, are common and widely distributed in the mountains. Others are seen less often: the Peaks of Otter salamander has not been discovered anywhere except in a small area surrounding its namesake summits (M.P. 86).

Like the aquatic salamanders, the woodland varieties subsist on invertebrates. If you look under a rock or a log searching for amphibians, you are likely to encounter their menu as well. Again, remember to replace any objects you move in order to preserve the animals' habitat (and keep in mind that plants and animals may not be collected along the Parkway).

Salamanders get a lot of attention in the southern Appalachians. Most of it comes not from Parkway visitors but from biologists. Researchers from all over the United States have studied one kind of salamander or another here, or made various careful comparisons among varieties. A major drawing force is the fact that the southern mountains have more kinds of salamanders than any other region in the world.

One major group, called the lungless salamanders, is believed by most

31. The pigmy salamander, identified by the row of small V's down its back, is found at high elevations along the North Carolina section of the Parkway.

researchers to have originated in the southern mountains. In the millions of years that have passed since they first evolved in the creeks of ancient Appalachia, members of this family have spread over much of the Western Hemisphere. The process of their development required suitable conditions and eons of time, and the southern Appalachians provided both.

What is intriguing to scientists is the fact that the lungless salamanders are evolving here still. Researchers find, for instance, that a Jordan's salamander on one mountain can be quite a bit different from one found a few summits away. Like the high-elevation spruce and firs, these salamanders are effectively trapped in isolated populations because of their need for special environmental conditions. In time, those in one place may evolve into an entirely different species from those in the other. Biologists hope to uncover evidence that this process is proceeding today.

Early spring rains initiate activities of frogs and toads as well as salamanders. Wood frogs, brown and masked like raccoons, are the first amphibians to emerge from winter dormancy. They aggregate in woodland pools and ponds in February to lay their eggs, even though ice and snow may still be on the ground. Then they return to the forest. Wood frogs spend the warm months away from water, living on the floor of moist woods below 4,000 feet in elevation.

It is March or April before other frogs appear in southern Appalachian lakes and ponds. The next to breed are the spring peepers. Identified as members of the treefrog family by the "suction cups" on the ends of their toes, peepers fill warm spring nights with their whistling calls. Despite being less than an inch and a half long, the spring peeper has a powerful voice, and large numbers of them can produce an almost deafening chorus. They seem at such times to be as thick as the leaves on the trees. Yet during the rest of the year, spring peepers are rarely seen. They spend the summer far above our heads, hunting insects in the forest canopy.

There are still spring peepers calling from Parkway ponds when the long, trilling voices of toads begin to ring in the evenings. Like wood frogs, toads visit bodies of water only to breed. During the warm months of the year, they hunt invertebrates on the forest floor or spend the hottest, driest periods buried in damp earth. Visitors occasionally encounter

32. People who roam the summer woods after soaking rains often find toads
hopping across the forest floor. During dry weather, however, toads
and most other amphibians are much less active.

toads after summer rains, when they are most active. Most predators leave toads alone, because the lumpy glands on the toad's skin secrete a poisonous fluid that irritates the soft membranes of an animal's mouth. Skunks, however, reportedly eat toads after first rubbing them on the ground to remove the poison. The hognose snake, moreover, feeds on little else; it is apparently unaffected by the toad's defense. (Handling toads will not give humans warts, but make sure to wash before putting your hands near your mouth.)

Mixed with the voices of peepers and toads in the spring are several less common species found in the mountains: cricket frogs, chorus frogs, and pickerel frogs all breed from March to May. The big lake and pond frogs don't begin to call, however, until spring fades into summer. It is then that the deep "jug-o-rum" of the bullfrog and the banjo-string twang of the green frog are heard. Unlike most other varieties found in the mountains, these live in water year round. There they feed on insects and —in the case of the larger bullfrog—on small fish, crayfish, and even an occasional young snake or bat. They in turn are caught by mink, raccoons, wading birds, large fish, snakes, and other predators.

Altogether, 14 kinds of frogs and toads occur in the southern mountains. To biological researchers, this group is not as significant as the salamanders, for several reasons. First, the environment is not quite so ideal for frogs and toads: they depend upon standing water for breeding, and lakes and ponds are rare here. Second, unlike salamanders, frogs and toads travel too easily to be isolated in small, disconnected populations; as a result, they do not provide the same opportunities to observe evolution in action.

Nonetheless, frogs and toads do play a significant part in the ecology of the mountains. And they may also make a welcome contribution to the vacation of a Parkway visitor who finds pleasure in the music of their voices on a warm June night.

Reptiles

The cool, moist weather that makes the southern Appalachians such a haven for amphibians has the opposite effect on reptiles. These animals are most at home in warm, generally dry conditions like those of the American Southwest. As a result the Blue Ridge and its sister ranges are not known for their reptiles, and many of the turtles, lizards, and snakes that do occur here are found only at low elevations. Still, nearly 40 reptiles are found at one place or another in the southern Appalachians, and the group is prominent both ecologically and in the minds of visitors.

If turtles are not the most familiar reptiles, certainly they are at least the most well regarded. People generally think of turtles – like the small ones formerly sold in the pet departments of dime stores – as slow-moving, docile creatures fond of quiet waters.

Along the Blue Ridge Parkway, however, quiet waters are in short supply, as are the kinds of turtles that inhabit them: local turtles do not fit the popular stereotype. The only species common to the lakes and ponds of the Parkway is the snapping turtle. Though snappers are generally found in quiet waters, there is nothing placid about their dispositions; perhaps as compensation for the skimpy protection their limited shells afford them, they have powerful jaws and bite savagely when provoked. Their jaws also aid them in their feeding, since they eat more animal foods than do most other turtles. Snapping turtles usually stay in the water. Occasionally, just their heads can be seen breaking the surface of Abbott Lake (M.P. 86), for instance, or Price Lake (M.P. 296.7); a casual observer might mistake them for stubs of small logs. In late spring and early summer, female snapping turtles wander into the woods to lay their eggs. During this period visitors sometimes encounter them on local roads. Don't poke or prod such a turtle; their jaws are not only sharp and strong but remarkably quick. I have seen snapping turtles along the Parkway that were well over a foot long, and I would hate to imagine the damage one could do to a human finger.

The other common turtle found in the southern Appalachians is the eastern box turtle. True to the general image, the box turtle has a very unaggressive personality, but it spends almost none of its time in water. Box turtles frequent the deciduous woods and can be found along the Parkway up to an elevation of about 4,500 feet. They are most active during the egg-laying season (June and early July). During the hot, dry periods of midsummer, they may remain very inactive, moving about only after rains. In the winter they hibernate under piles of forest debris and in soft earth.

Almost any plant or animal material satisfies the hunger of the box turtle: it eats insects, earthworms, wild strawberries, other wild fruits,

and even poisonous mushrooms. Adult turtles have practically no predators, protected as they are by hard shells with hinged flaps that allow the
animal to seal its head and tail inside. The slow-moving box turtle's most
significant enemies are speeding automobiles (care should be taken to
avoid hitting them when they are on the roadway) and forest fires.

Several other turtles inhabit the larger streams and rivers passing under the Parkway, but visitors are not likely to see them. One more found
here is of interest, though: the rare bog turtle occurs in a few isolated col-
onies in wet meadows, sluggish streams, and boggy areas. Like the red
spruce, paper birch, and many other plants and animals of the southern
Appalachians, the bog turtle is now primarily a northern species, left
stranded on high elevations by the retreat of the glaciers. Along the Parkway, populations of bog turtles are known to exist near Price Park (M.P. 296.7)
and in small areas both north and south of Mabry Mill (M.P. 176.2).

Of the reptiles found in the southern Appalachians, visitors are least
likely to notice the lizards. A half-dozen varieties live in the mountains
along the Parkway's route, but most of them only at the lowest elevations.

Only two lizards can be considered common here: the eastern fence
lizard and the five-lined skink. Fence lizards are most likely to be found
in dry, sunny woods, where they search for large insects, spiders, snails,
and other invertebrates. Hikers will occasionally surprise one as it suns
itself on a warm rock. Typically, the fence lizard escapes with a quick
dash to a nearby tree, where—like a squirrel—it will remain motionless
on the side opposite the intruder. Eastern fence lizards have rough brown
skin with dark bars across the back, and are generally five or six inches
long. The five-lined skink is about the same size but can be easily identified by the pattern of light and dark lines that run from its nose to the
base of its tail. In addition, the tails of young skinks are a bright blue.
The skink has a diet similar to that of the fence lizard but generally lives
in moister areas.

Both reptiles are found to at least 4,000 feet, but are less common as
elevation increases. Should you spot one during a visit to the mountains,
please do not make a grab for it. Fence lizards and skinks are completely
harmless; the concern is not that they will injure you but rather that you
will do them damage. Both lizards have detachable tails, and a sudden
pull on one will cause it to break off. You will be left with a wiggling tail
in your hand and a stunned look on your face, and the lizard will have

lost one of its primary survival aids. Should it meet a predator before re-growing the lost tail, its chances of escaping will be reduced. Observe and enjoy Parkway wildlife, therefore, but do not harass it.

The last group of southern Appalachian reptiles remaining to be discussed is the snakes. No category of animals—with the possible exception of bears—seems to excite so many people to such a great degree. This has been the case throughout history and is certainly as true in the southern mountains as anywhere else. Folklore and legend abound: people have been told that certain snakes can stand on their tails and whistle, that others will grab their tails in their mouths and roll like hoops, and that black snakes and copperheads sometimes mate (producing, the inference is, litters of venomous black snakes). As a result of the general prejudice against snakes, they have in many areas been reduced in numbers by well-meaning but misinformed people. The Blue Ridge Parkway, happily, is a preserve where snakes, as much as any other wildlife, are protected.

Part of the interest in snakes stems from the fact that certain species are venomous and can therefore pose a threat to humans. This is a legitimate concern along the Parkway, for two venomous varieties do occur here. However, the rare visitor who does encounter a snake during his stay in the southern Appalachians can be fairly well assured that it will be one of the 21 harmless kinds found here.

There are perhaps four species of snakes more frequently seen on Parkway hiking trails than any others. All are harmless. In my experience, the most common is the black rat snake. (This species and the black racer are lumped together as "black snakes" by most residents of the Southeast.) Coming upon one by surprise can be shocking to someone not familiar with them. Rat snakes grow quite large (specimens five and six feet long are not uncommon) and frequently stand their ground when threatened by an intruding human. In addition, this is one of several nonvenomous snakes that will coil up and vibrate its tail in the dry leaves at such times, producing a sound disconcertingly like the rattlesnake's warning buzz. To round off its exhibition, a black rat snake may then turn and escape by climbing straight up the trunk of a nearby tree.

Despite all this drama, though, the rat snake's life history is unexcep-

33. The black rat snake is fairly common in the mountains. It feeds
primarily on mice, swallowing them whole as all snakes do.

tional among southern Appalachian snakes. Black rat snakes live throughout the area's deciduous forests and feed mainly on mice. They lay from
5 to 25 eggs in June or July, usually in rotting wood or piles of forest debris. Young rat snakes, like the hatchlings of many other species, emerge in
late summer or fall. On their route to adulthood, many are eaten by
predators.

Probably the most abundant snake in the southern Appalachians is
the ringneck snake; because of its secretive habits, however, the little
ringneck frequently escapes the attention of visitors. This species occurs
at all but the highest elevations. Individuals are most active at night,
when they hunt earthworms, salamanders, and other small animals on
the forest floor. Ringneck snakes rarely grow longer than 18 inches and
are harmless.

The eastern garter snake is also common along the Parkway. Individuals vary, but usually they are dark with indistinct yellow stripes. The
garter snake is recognized by many people, for the species is found all
over the eastern United States, even in vacant city lots. In the southern
mountains garter snakes prefer to live near streams or in wet meadows,
where they feed mostly on small frogs, toads and earthworms. They release a strong-smelling musk when molested, but despite this defense
many are eaten by skunks, raccoons, hawks and even other snakes.

Observant visitors who frequent trails near water, like the Otter
Creek Trail (M.P. 60.8) and those around Abbott Lake (M.P. 86) and
Price Lake (M.P. 296.7), are likely to run across the northern water
snake. Fairly large and dark, these harmless serpents are often misidenti-
fied as the venomous cottonmouth, or "water moccasin." The cottonmouth,
however, is an inhabitant of wet lowland areas only, and does not occur
within 100 miles of the Blue Ridge Parkway. Water snakes will bite if ha-
rassed, grabbed, or cornered, but their short, needlelike teeth—like those
of all nonvenomous snakes—are incapable of doing much damage to humans. They are much better suited to catching the water snake's natural
food: fish, crayfish, frogs, and salamanders.

The two venomous snakes found in the southern Appalachians—
which, by their very existence, have kept more people from enjoying
these woods than any other animal—are the copperhead and the timber
rattlesnake. They can be quickly distinguished from all of the region's
harmless snakes, however, by their triangular heads and thin necks.

Copperheads are the more numerous of the two species. These snakes inhabit a number of different habitats, but in the mountains seem to occur most often on rocky slopes, in loose rock walls, near woodland streams, and around abandoned buildings. (Visitors should be particularly careful in such areas, especially since they are also the preferred haunts of rattlesnakes.) The copperhead is a tan color marked with darker hourglass designs, and the resulting pattern renders it practically invisible in the dead leaves of the forest floor. Adults usually measure 24 to 30 inches in length. When threatened or stepped on, copperheads do not hesitate to bite, but they do not (as some visitors fear) attack or chase people. Their main foods are mice, frogs, insects, and other small animals. Since they are primarily active at night, these snakes are rarely seen; in my years of hiking Parkway trails, I have yet to encounter one there. I have observed copperheads only on the road after dark, where they sometimes lie to absorb the warmth that lingers in the pavement.

Timber rattlesnakes are larger than copperheads; big ones can be over four feet long, but adults are more commonly about three feet. In the mountains these snakes occur in two color phases: some are yellow with irregular black bands and blotches; others are almost completely black. The dark phase is more prevalent at high elevations; it may be that darker skin allows these snakes to take full advantage of the heat of the sun, giving them a survival edge on the cooler mountain summits. At all elevations, the rattler's chief prey is rodents. By injecting a mouse with venom, the snake avoids the risk of having to engage it in what might be a damaging battle. The rattlesnake's poisonous bite is used in defense only as a last resort.

Many visitors are concerned about the threat these venomous snakes pose to them and their children. Certainly, persons hiking and camping in areas where rattlesnakes and copperheads occur should not behave recklessly; they should watch where they walk and not put their hands into cracks and crevices where snakes may be concealed. However, the danger venomous snakes pose to people in the woods is often greatly exaggerated, and fear should certainly not keep you in your car.

Approximately 9,000 people are bitten by venomous snakes each year in the United States, with about 15 consequent fatalities. Most of the deaths are caused by big diamondback rattlesnakes, which are not found in the Blue Ridge. Deaths resulting from timber rattlesnake bites are very

34. The vision of a coiled rattlesnake is seen far more often in Hollywood
movies than in real life. Shy and relatively inactive during the day,
timber rattlesnakes are rarely encountered by visitors.

unusual, and fatalities caused by copperheads are almost unknown. The Blue Ridge Parkway, despite hosting millions of visitors each year, has recorded only a handful of venomous snakebites in its history; none has been fatal.

The danger of snakebite can be likened to that of being struck by lightning. Both are rare happenings in nature, and both can be avoided with a few simple precautions.

It is unfortunate that snakes must suffer so undeserved a reputation. Throughout its range, for example, the timber rattlesnake has been significantly reduced in numbers during the past few decades. This reduction has been due in large part to encroachment on its habitat, but many are also killed by people who neglect to realize that rattlers play an important role in the ecology of the forest. The fact that rattlesnakes and their relatives still live unmolested in the sanctuary of our National Parks should serve to remind us of an important point: an animal's level of importance in the natural world is not related to whether or not we like it.

Birds

Early on a quiet, sunny morning I pulled my car into the parking lot of the Mount Pisgah picnic area (M.P. 407.8). I walked up the trail and into the woods. It was late June, and the flame azaleas were at the peak of their blooming. I was not there to admire the flowers, however. With my beat-up old binoculars around my neck, I was looking for birds.

Actually, the best and easiest time to watch birds in the southern Appalachians is in late April and May. This is the peak of the spring migration season, and the woods are full of birds headed north. Many of them are species that do not nest in the southern mountains; they can be seen only as they pass through. In addition, because the leaves have not yet fully emerged on the trees at this time, the birds are a lot easier to spot.

I had purposely waited until late June. The fact that the migrant birds had already come and gone was fine with me. I was interested in the ones that had stayed to nest.

"Zoo-zee, zoo-zoo-zee!"

I cocked my head to listen. Once the forest canopy is thick with greenery, the best way to locate birds is to hear them. This songster I recognized as a black-throated green warbler, a small, active insect-eater more colorful than its name implies. I couldn't find him, though ("him," because in almost all bird species only the male sings). The bird was high in a tree some 20 or 30 yards in, and the leaves shielded him from view. I kept walking.

A little farther on I was startled by another bird; it burst from the vegetation right next to me, flew to the foot of a yellow birch immediately ahead, and hopped about nervously, chirping. The bird was a dark-eyed junco—a "snowbird" to local people, because it is so commonly seen in winter. "Am I near its nest?" I wondered. It seemed a reasonable assumption from the way the junco was acting, and I searched briefly near the spot where it had popped out of the flowers—on the ground, which is where juncos invariably build the grassy cups that cradle their eggs. No luck, though. I gave up quickly, not wanting to disturb the parents too much. It was enough to know that the nest was somewhere near.

Along a service road on the south side of the picnic area are some small fire cherry trees. In late June the fruit was already beginning to ripen. There I was delighted to find a male rose-breasted grosbeak, so busy gorging himself on cherries that he seemed not to notice me. Particularly when enlarged in binoculars, the grosbeak is a striking bird— black above and white below, with a vibrant red "bib" on its breast. To mask dribbled cherry juice, perhaps, I mused.

Then, only ten feet ahead, a small bird fluttered in to land on a low branch. It was a Canada warbler. No doubt I broke into a grin. Not only is the gray, black, and yellow Canada warbler one of my favorite birds; it also epitomizes the first part of the story this chapter strives to tell—the story of the special nature of southern Appalachian birdlife.

Birds of the North

The story should be growing familiar: among southern Appalachian birds, as is true of the plants, invertebrates, fish, amphibians, and reptiles already discussed, there are a number of species ordinarily associated with the northern United States and Canada. When the great spring waves of migrating birds wash over the mountains on their way to the forests of Ontario, New England, and upstate New York, pools and pockets of northern varieties remain behind. Their migration has ended; they build their nests, lay their eggs, and raise their young on mountaintops in the southern Appalachians.

Altogether, about 20 percent of the bird species that breed in these mountains are types more commonly found in the North. At high elevations in the Blue Ridge and its neighboring ranges, the cool temperatures, northern forests, and northern insects and food plants duplicate in many ways the usual homes of these birds. As a result, the birdwatcher from Atlanta who has never been to Canada need not drive 800 miles to discover its birdlife. He or she can sally out into the nearby Smokies or the southern Blue Ridge, see a dozen or more northern species, and be home before dark.

The Canada warbler is a typical example of the region's northern birds. It is common in the spruce and fir forests of Ontario, Quebec, the northern tier of Great Lakes states, and New England, where it nests in the forest undergrowth. Along the Parkway, Canada warblers can be found above an elevation of about 3,500 feet. They especially like to re-

side near water, in second-growth thickets and tangles of rhododendron.
There the birds are active in low branches, where they hunt insects to
feed themselves and their young. Canada warblers can be found not only
on Mount Pisgah but at most of the Parkway's other North Carolina rec-

35. High in the mountains, juncos build nests on the ground under grasses and other vegetation. Elsewhere in the south they are only winter visitors.

reation areas: try the woods around Trout Lake at Moses Cone Park
(M.P. 294), or Craggy Gardens (M.P. 364.6). Canada warblers are less
frequently seen along the Virginia section of the Parkway, where elevations are lower, but some do nest on the high slopes of the Peaks of Otter
(M.P. 85.9) and around Rocky Knob (M.P. 169).

The list of other northern birds occurring in the southern mountains
is long. The names of the birds I encountered at Mount Pisgah are all on
it: the black-throated green warbler, the dark-eyed junco, the rose-breasted
grosbeak. So are the names of many other warblers, plus the golden-
crowned kinglet, the red-breasted nuthatch, and the veery. The ranges of
most of these birds reach down from the north in a more or less continuous belt along the Appalachians. A few, however, occur (like spruce and
fir) in isolated spots scattered across the highest summits. The black-
capped chickadee, for instance, is limited to high elevations in the
Smokies, Balsams, and Great Balsams; this is as far south as it occurs in
North America. (Its look-alike cousin the Carolina chickadee is common
here, however.) Another example is the tiny saw-whet owl, which can be
found during the breeding season on Mount Mitchell (M.P. 355.3), Richland Balsam (M.P. 431.4), and other summits covered by Canadian-zone
forests. To the north, the next place it inhabits is central West Virginia.
And perhaps most remarkable is the case of the raven. Large crowlike
birds found around the windy cliffs and outcrops of the highest mountains, the ravens of the southern Appalachian region are separated from
their relatives in Canada by a gap of well over 400 miles.

Of interest to ornithologists (biologists who specialize in birds) is the
fact that many of the mountains' northern birds live in surroundings different from those they choose in Canada. Some of the warblers, for instance, prefer evergreen shrubs for their nesting in the North, yet are sat-
isfied with thickets of chestnut saplings here in the southern Appalachians. What is the significance of this difference? It may merely indicate
that the birds are more flexible than we thought. On the other hand, it
may mean that the Canada warbler of the Appalachians is no longer
quite the same kind of bird as the Canada warbler of central Ontario;
through time, environmental pressures may be slowly modifying the two
separate populations. They are not radically altered yet, but certain
southern Appalachian birds – juncos, song sparrows, ruffed grouse, and
others – already differ from their northern counterparts in some recogniz-

able ways. Whether or not they are to become new species, only the next million or so years of evolution will tell.

One Day of Birds

Though there are inconveniences associated with camping along the Blue Ridge Parkway (like the lack of hot showers), there are benefits as well. One of them is the opportunity to wake in the morning to the sounds of birds.

If you can identify bird songs, you will realize before you leave your sleeping bag that, in addition to northern varieties, the Parkway has many avian residents common all over the Southeast. In some campgrounds it will be a robin that wakes you. In others the cardinal is the first to sing. And if it is still early in the summer, more than a dozen kinds of birds will be in full voice by the time the campground's first bacon is frying.

Birds are most active early in the cool hours of the morning, so visitors who would like to see them are advised to be active then, too. Take a walk before nine o'clock, and if at all possible carry binoculars with you. With the aid of their magnification, you should be able to find 15 or 20 kinds of birds even on an average morning.

Many of the Parkway's most prevalent birds can be identified without a guidebook even by novice birdwatchers. The majority of visitors are familiar with the robins, cardinals, crows, and bluejays that are common in most Parkway recreation areas. The rufous-sided towhee is another bird frequently seen and easily identified. It is often found in campgrounds and other areas where thick underbrush occurs. A towhee is about the size of a robin. Males are black above, white underneath, and have a rusty streak down either side; females (less frequently seen because much of their summer is spent with the young) have the same pattern, but the black feathers are replaced with brown. Also in brushy areas at the woods' edge will be the catbird, a slate-gray relative of the mockingbird.

If your walk takes you near a stream, you may encounter the eastern phoebe. The phoebe is a seven-inch-long flycatcher with a habit of "wagging" its tail and a penchant for nesting under bridges. Its persistent call of "fee-bee, fee-bee" catches the ear of many visitors (including one who once inquired what bird it was that kept crying, "Feed me!").

36. The wood thrush is common in deciduous woods throughout the southeastern United States. Its flutelike song is often heard just at dusk.

37. The veery, a close relative of the wood thrush, tends to replace it
in the forests of the highest southern Appalachian peaks.

38. The robin is a Blue Ridge resident familiar to everyone.

Your walk finished and breakfast eaten, you pull out for another day's traveling. Even when you are driving along the Parkway, some birds will be easy to spot. Most conspicuous are the turkey vultures, dark soaring birds with a wingspread so large (six feet from wing tip to wing tip) that many people mistake them for eagles. Vultures drift along the ridges, buoyed by warm midday air currents, and keep alert for the road-killed squirrel or groundhog that will be their next meal. With luck you may see a red-tailed hawk aloft as well. The hawk's light-colored undersides distinguish it from the vultures.

Along some sections of the Parkway, eastern bluebirds can still be found. These birds, which prefer a mixture of open farm country and woods, have greatly decreased in numbers during the last century, in large part as a result of competition with introduced house sparrows and starlings. Particularly in the area around Roanoke (M.P. 112.2), however, they are relatively common. Much of the credit for this goes to the Roanoke Valley Bird Club, which builds and maintains bluebird houses along this stretch of the Parkway.

Visitors who spot a bird that is entirely blue will probably have encountered the indigo bunting. (Bluebirds, in contrast, have rusty orange breasts like robins.) Buntings are typically found wherever forest and field meet. In addition, they are one of the few birds that remain active through the heat of a summer afternoon.

Back in a campground for the evening, you will hear a twilight chorus usher in the darkness. In the lower-elevation campgrounds (like Otter Creek, M.P. 60.8), the flutelike notes of the wood thrush will be the last heard. At higher elevations the wood thrush will be joined by its northern cousin, the veery. By the time the stars appear, the woods will be quiet – that is, unless the owls provide a reprise. Most common along the Parkway are the screech owl, a small bird with an eerie cry reminiscent of a whinnying horse, and the larger barred owl, which drawls with southern flavor, "Who-cooks-for-you? Who-cooks-for-you-all-l-l?" Especially around the pastures and fields of the central section of the Parkway, the great horned owl adds its melancholy hooting to the night sounds.

This morning-to-evening listing includes the commoner Parkway birds. In the course of a day's searching, a diligent visitor might find many more; in all, 159 species of birds are known to nest in the southern Appalachians, and during the migration seasons (April–May and Septem-

39. The thick forests of southern Appalachian coves and hollows are a favorite haunt of the barred owl.

ber–October), dozens more pass through. Moreover, every recreation area along the Blue Ridge Parkway has a somewhat different complement of resident birds, because each one provides them with different elevations and different habitats. So take along a pair of binoculars and a good bird book, and see what you can find.

The Mountains' Other Influences

In addition to having preserved northern living conditions for northern birds, the southern Appalachians have had several other effects on the region's birdlife.

One is obvious, yet easy to overlook: by discouraging farming and (to a certain extent) logging, the rugged southern Appalachians have retained the forests that many birds require for their survival. A prime example is the wild turkey. A bird that prefers mature forests interspersed with clearings, the turkey was nearly eliminated from both Virginia and North Carolina by 1900. Even in the mountains, its numbers dwindled to nearly nothing as a result of logging and hunting. Since early in this century, however, the forests have been returning, and so have the wild turkeys. Now they are locally common, especially along the Virginia section of the Parkway in areas like Humpback Rocks (M.P. 5.8) and the Peaks of Otter (M.P. 85.9). Turkeys may be encountered in the warmer months in large family flocks—chasing grasshoppers in a field, perhaps, or scratching beneath oak trees in search of acorns.

Other birds are similarly dependent upon the extensive southern Appalachian forests. The ruffed grouse thrives along the Parkway, particularly where second-growth timber provides it with plentiful food and thick cover. The pileated woodpecker—a striking black, white, and red bird the size of a crow—can live only where the trees are large enough to contain its sizable nesting and roosting cavities; such stands of trees are common in the southern mountains.

At least one bird requires not forest but wilderness—an area undisturbed by roads, farms, power saws, or shotguns. This is the golden eagle. Once residents of most of North America, golden eagles disappeared as humans advanced, until today they cling to the most remote areas of the West and to just a handful of cliff faces in the northern Appalachians of New England. No nests have been found in the southern

40. In many areas along the Parkway, the wild turkey – once rare – can now be found in large numbers.

41. Ruffed grouse are occasionally seen along the roadway, especially in the late spring. Reluctant to fly, they are sometimes hit by cars.

Appalachians in recent years, but golden eagles have continued to appear here sporadically. Is it possible that this, the largest of our continent's predatory birds, may still be able to live and breed in the southern mountains? Perhaps. In an effort to restore them to the Blue Ridge, an alliance of state and federal agencies and private groups has begun to release young birds here. The hope is that they will remain, eventually to nest in the region and add their own young to a growing eagle population. Watch for golden eagles in the vicinity of Graveyard Fields (M.P. 418.8), along the highest and most rugged stretch of the Parkway in North Carolina.

Some birds are influenced by the mountains only during migration. For many species, the airspace above the Blue Ridge Parkway serves as a sort of aerial highway, as they follow the Appalachian ridges north in the spring and south in the fall. Birds rely on a number of cues to help them find their way to and from their nesting grounds, and it may be that the same landmarks that capture the attention of visitors are important guideposts to migrating birds.

During the spring, birds travel in sporadic hops. Each time a warm air mass surges northward from the Gulf of Mexico, thousands of birds take to the skies, pushed ahead by strong tailwinds. When the warm air collides with an approaching cold front, the birds land in the forest and feed, waiting for their next boost north. This is the best time to see them; concentrations of a whole range of species may be found in a relatively small area.

The fall migration to a great extent is the same process in reverse: birds ride cold fronts like surfers, then land when winds change. However, the autumn migration seems to be less dramatic. The birds' southward travel is more leisurely; the bright colors of their spring breeding plumage are gone; and there is little singing.

In general, visitors pay less attention to birds at this time – except for those interested in hawks. For hawks display the opposite pattern: they migrate inconspicuously in the spring, but come autumn they pour southward along the Appalachian ridges in flocks.

Like other birds, hawks travel with the weather. Their requirements, however, are somewhat different: hawks benefit not only from northerly winds, but from sunshine. Warm rays of the sun heat cliffs and rock outcroppings along the Blue Ridge and parallel ranges. The heated rocks, in turn, warm the air above them, which rises in forceful drafts called "thermals." Hawks, soaring and spiraling on motionless wings, rise with those drafts. Eventually the air currents cool and cease to provide the birds lift; by this time, however, the hawks are thousands of feet in the air. They turn, and drift southward in long glides toward the next updraft. In this manner hawks can travel hundreds of miles in a day.

There is much interest in watching the fall hawk migration along the Parkway, especially in Virginia, north of Roanoke. There, hawks concentrate above the one long spine of the Blue Ridge, and on the best days in mid- and late-September, visitors can watch hundreds drift by in an afternoon. Rockfish Gap (M.P. 0), Buena Vista Overlook (M.P. 45.6), and Harvey's Knob Overlook (M.P. 95.3) are all prime hawk-watching locations. Along the North Carolina section of the Parkway, try Craggy Pinnacle (M.P. 364.1), Mills Valley Overlook (M.P. 404.5), and Devil's Courthouse (M.P. 422.4). Broad-winged hawks are the most common transients, but visitors with fortunate timing may see birds as rare as the peregrine falcon (and perhaps even the bald eagle).

If you are traveling along the Parkway in the fall, take a break from driving and spend some time watching for hawks. In the quiet of an autumn afternoon, perhaps no scene so well sums up the essence of the relationship between mountains and birds as the view of a hawk gliding smoothly off into a landscape of rolling, blue-green hills.

Mammals

"Are there any bears around here?"

If it is summer, chances are that somewhere in our national park system a visitor is asking this question of a ranger right now. National parks have come to be nearly synonymous with mammals, especially big mammals, and we all hope to see something worth writing the neighbors about. Will we encounter a moose standing majestically in an Isle Royale lake? Mountain goats on a rocky ridge of Washington's Olympic Peninsula? Or—a bear?

This is no remote, sprawling wilderness, however. The Blue Ridge Parkway is only a three-hour drive from Washington, D.C., and Atlanta. Are there any bears around *here*?

Yes, there are. Despite being so close to so many millions of people, the southern Appalachians are home to several large mammals as well as a host of smaller ones. A now familiar pattern is evidenced in the mammals, too: with 90 species known to have occurred here in historic times, the southern Appalachians accommodate more kinds of mammals than any other area of eastern North America.

The fact may not be obvious. Very few visitors see bears along the Blue Ridge Parkway; there are only a few hundred of them, and bears are generally secretive animals. Very few visitors see (or even think about) mice or shrews while they are here. They too are secretive, but in contrast to bears, there are literally millions of mice and shrews in the southern Appalachians. They outnumber all the other mammals combined.

This chapter will introduce you to the furred residents of the southern Appalachians—not only the large, celebrated mammals that are always the subject of much attention but the small, easily overlooked ones as well. The level of an animal's popularity is not necessarily an index of its significance in nature.

History of Blue Ridge Mammals

National park visitors were not the first group of people for whom large mammals held great interest. Native Americans living in the southern Appalachians before the time of Columbus hunted the animals for food and clothing, and when the first Europeans arrived in the late 1600s, they also relied on big game for their survival.

William Byrd, Daniel Boone, and other early explorers found animals in the Blue Ridge never seen here today. Then, buffalo, elk, and white-tailed deer ate the abundant mountain vegetation and were hunted by timber wolves and mountain lions. The southern Appalachian region formed a wilderness measured not in acres but in thousands of square miles. And because the mountains were far less hospitable than the rich river valleys, they remained wild longer. But eventually even this rugged vastness drew civilized attention. Once the good, flat lands were all taken, settlers moved up the steep slopes and into the Blue Ridge. Populations of the large mammals dwindled, driven back by rifle, ax, and plow.

Several species eventually disappeared. The woodland buffalo, cousin to the bison of the western plains, was first to go; the last recorded sighting was around 1800. Buffalo were probably never numerous, but some areas had at least small populations. One buffalo trail existing into the early 1700s crossed the Blue Ridge at Rockfish Gap (now the northern terminus of the Parkway), and Bull Gap (M.P. 375.3) is said to have been named for the last buffalo killed in the Asheville area.

The next large mammal to become extinct in the southern Appalachians was the American elk, or wapiti. In the same family as the white-tailed deer, elk grow four or five times as big; some reach 1,000 pounds. They were found in the Appalachians while wilderness persisted but were exterminated in the North Carolina mountains shortly after the buffalo. In Virginia, elk held on somewhat longer, but the last native specimen on record was shot in 1855. Elk Valley (seen from M.P. 281.2) and the towns of Elk Park and Banner Elk (near the Grandfather Mountain section of the Parkway) commemorate this animal.

The wolf and mountain lion rely principally on large hoofed mammals for food; thus as the numbers of deer, buffalo, and elk dwindled, their predators also fell on hard times. The fact that some predators found hogs and sheep a good alternative food source turned every farmer's rifle against them, and the results of this conflict were inevitable: after 1855, mountain lions were no longer found in the Blue Ridge, and wolves had followed them into oblivion by the time the century closed.

What has happened to the smaller mammals in the last 300 years is

Tom R. Johnson

not well documented. For the most part, animals not big enough to feed settlers' families or kill livestock were not big enough to make history. Though their relative numbers have no doubt changed through time — particularly because of man-made alterations in their forest habitat — probably only a few small mammals have disappeared from the Blue Ridge. Some, like the porcupine and the marten, were rare to begin with.

The Large Mammals of Today

The white-tailed deer is the only large mammal visitors to the Blue Ridge Parkway are likely to see. Although deer appear infrequently along many sections of the Parkway, in areas like Humpback Rocks (M.P. 5.8), the Peaks of Otter (M.P. 85.9), and Doughton Park (M.P. 241.1) they are plentiful enough to be not only a treat but a traffic hazard. Several dozen deer are hit by automobiles every year on the Parkway despite the relatively low speed limit.

The visitor who counts six or eight deer during a brief evening drive through the Doughton Park picnic area may find it hard to believe that the whitetails nearly followed their cousins the elks into oblivion along the Blue Ridge. Although fairly numerous in the days of the Cherokee, by the early 1900s deer were virtually unknown in the mountains. Their homes had been destroyed by lumbering and farming; many had been shot by southern Appalachian settlers; and "their worst enemy the roving, self-hunting dog"[1] had chased down and killed great numbers. However, circumstances began to change just as the deer population reached critically low levels. Abandoned farmlands and barren logged areas began to grow back, sprouting up into the dense, brushy thickets that make excellent deer habitat. Laws were enacted that restricted hunting. Deer from other regions were released in the mountains by private clubs and state game agencies. The white-tailed deer recovered so well that it is now more common in the southern Appalachians than it ever was, and the chances of seeing one of these graceful animals are markedly better for today's visitor than they were for the mountaineer of 50 years ago.

To better the odds, it is helpful to know something of deer behavior.

1. Charles O. Handley, Jr., and Clyde P. Patton, *Wild Mammals of Virginia* (Commonwealth of Virginia, Commission of Game and Inland Fisheries, 1947).

42. White-tailed deer can sometimes be seen crossing the Parkway, especially in the early mornings or late evenings.

Whitetails generally feed from evening until the early morning hours, and these are the best times to spot them. You can watch for deer as you drive along the Parkway, but to see them while you are hiking can be even more satisfying—and is certainly more challenging. Always alert for possible danger, the white-tailed deer has an excellent sense of smell, acute hearing, and eyes that quickly spot moving objects. The hiker's best strategy is to walk quietly, keep alert, and "freeze" when a deer appears.

The black bear, which occasionally reaches 400 pounds in the mountains, is the largest animal still found in the Blue Ridge. While many other large mammals were disappearing, bears clung tenaciously to their mountain retreats. At home in the steepest, rockiest terrain, easily able to fight off loose dogs, and willing to eat almost anything, bears persisted where less flexible mammals did not. As a result, mountain lore is filled with stories of encounters with bears, and the animal has left a legacy of colorful names up and down the ridge: Bear Pen Gap (M.P. 427.6), Bear Trail Ridge (M.P. 430.4), Bear Den Overlook (M.P. 323.1), and two Bearwallow Gaps (M.P. 90.5 and M.P. 335.4) all commemorate the black bear.

The variety of foods a bear will eat is impressive. It is generally known that black bears like berries, grubs, and honey, but these are just tidbits on the long menu of bear meals. Dining begins in earnest in early spring, when warming weather stimulates the bruin's hunger. Nature provides young grasses at this time, and occasionally carcasses of animals that have died during the winter. A few more warm weeks pass, and soon there are enough insects around to make a meal. Ants are a favorite food, and bears also seem to relish digging up yellow jacket nests and eating the larvae inside. I once watched a small cub have what was perhaps its first encounter with yellow jackets. Alerted by the smell of something edible, it dug excitedly into the ground. Predictably, the angry wasps swarmed out. The first sting on its nose seemed to surprise the bear cub considerably; it jumped back, but quickly returned to finish digging out the nest. (The thick fur of bears seems to protect the rest of their bodies from insect stings.)

When summer brings wild cherries, black bears will climb up into the trees and rip down branches to get at the ripe fruits. By the time fall arrives, bears will have sampled nearly everything in the woods. In addition to the items already mentioned, snakes, frogs, salamanders, mushrooms, mice, roots, chipmunks, woodchucks, crayfish, and many other animal and vegetable materials will have passed down their throats. And as winter approaches, they eat great quantities of acorns in a final effort to build up the large fat deposits that must last them through the cold weather to the next spring.

Bears are popularly thought to hibernate during the winter, but in fact they do not. True hibernation involves dramatic bodily changes in a mammal: heart rate slows to only a beat or two per minute, and body temperature drops significantly. Among the mammals found along the Blue Ridge Parkway, only woodchucks, chipmunks, jumping mice, and some of the bats are true hibernators. During the harshest weather bears will find a protected place and sleep (sometimes for weeks), but their bodily functions slow down only slightly. Black bears in the southern Appalachians may remain active all winter: I have seen bear tracks in the snow at Craggy Gardens (M.P. 364.6) in January.

It should be pointed out that bears, although at least sometimes present in most areas of the Blue Ridge, are rarely seen by visitors and—happily—almost never in Parkway camping areas. (The Mount Pisgah campground gets an occasional visit.) Faced with hunting pressures whenever they wander from the protection of National Park Service land, most bears retain a healthy fear of humans. Still, visitors should always take precautions and not leave food accessible in camp. (And do keep in mind how many things mean "food" to the black bear.)

Several other large mammals are found in the southern mountains. The largest bona fide predator prowling here (unless there are still mountain lions) is the bobcat. Weighing an average of 20 to 25 pounds, this animal survives partly because of its fondness for the rocky, broken country that farmers never clear and hunters rarely venture into. Bobcats are meat-eaters, and the fact that they will occasionally attack and kill small or weakened deer makes them the only natural predator still helping to keep whitetail populations in check. The bulk of their diet, however, consists of squirrels, rabbits, mice, and birds. Bobcats inhabit terrain along the entire length of the Parkway (except in populated areas), but because of their nocturnal habits and extreme wariness, only the luckiest visitor gets more than a fleeting glimpse of one.

Two aquatic mammals are rare but occasionally found in the southern Appalachians: the beaver and the otter. Both prefer sizable streams to live in, and their habitat requirements are not met in many places along the Parkway. Beaver have been observed in recent years around Otter Lake (M.P. 63.1), but otter are at best very infrequent visitors here. (The names Otter Creek, M.P. 60.8, and the Peaks of Otter, M.P. 85.9, may testify that the animals were more common at one time.)

Smaller Blue Ridge Mammals

Campers who hear the rustling sounds of animals at night may fear that large beasts stand nearly shoulder to shoulder in the Blue Ridge forests. In fact, most of the mammals found in the mountains (and heard at night) are relatively small.

There are many aspects of the smaller mammals that merit attention, but probably the most notable thing about them is the great diversity of their forms. To the casual observer, one kind of fish seems pretty much like another, and there are no strikingly visible differences in the structures of various salamanders. But ask even a young child how a rabbit differs from a skunk, and you will get a knowledgeable response. These differences are not the result of coincidence or chance. The rabbit's large ears and the skunk's odor help each animal to survive, and to live in a unique way. Special colors, structures, and types of behavior are known as adaptations, and though all plants and animals (including fish and salamanders) have their own adaptations, perhaps no group displays such a diverse and easily observed array as the small mammals.

Probably the one most frequently seen along the Blue Ridge Parkway is the woodchuck (or groundhog, as it is known in the mountains). Woodchucks make their homes in fields, overlooks, and roadside bays the length of the Parkway. Visitors encounter them often, not only because they live near the roadway but also because – unlike many mammals – woodchucks are active during the day. If you spot a chubby rodent sitting up alertly on its haunches or dashing clumsily across the road in front of you, feel confident that you have seen a woodchuck.

Possessing short legs and hampered by heavy layers of fat, the woodchuck would seem to be poorly designed to survive in an area where quick foxes and hungry bobcats prowl. However, a stout body shape is actually a boon to the groundhog. Its strong limbs and claws allow it to dig long, deep systems of tunnels; instead of running from predators, it dives into a nearby burrow. Its large fat deposits allow it to hibernate through the winter, sometimes remaining dormant for four months or more. And the sacrifice in speed is not of any great importance to the woodchuck's feeding: a vegetarian, it eats mainly grasses.

Woodchucks do not always escape their predators. Foxes and bobcats occasionally catch them off guard, and black bears have been known to dig them out of their tunnels. Like every other living thing, the wood-chuck has its place in the food web. And woodchucks make another con-tribution to the forest community: their vacant burrows are often used by other animals.

The cottontail rabbit is a primary beneficiary of such ready-made shelters, using them especially as protection from bad weather. Rabbits, too, eat grasses and other plant materials, and as a result have teeth gen-erally similar to the woodchuck's. Their other adaptations are quite a bit different, however. The cottontail escapes from predators by detecting them early with its acute hearing and sense of smell, then relying – when it needs to – on its quickness and agility. The cottontail's large ears and powerful hind legs are clues to its life-style.

There are in fact two species of these rabbits in the Blue Ridge: the eastern cottontail, common throughout the eastern United States and fa-miliar to many people, and the New England cottontail. As its name im-plies, the latter is a northern animal, appearing in Virginia and North Carolina only in the highest sections of mountains. The two species look almost identical, so visitors are unlikely to be able to tell them apart. In Virginia, New England cottontails predominate at elevations over 3,000 feet; in North Carolina they probably live higher. One physical difference between the two species is that the New England cottontail has smaller ears. Smaller ears mean less skin exposed to the air, which may give it an advantage on the mountaintops, where winter is most severe and body heat most easily lost.

Muskrats might be looked for around the James River (M.P. 63.6), at Julian Price Park (M.P. 296.7), Linville Falls Campground (M.P. 316.4), Mabry Mill (M.P. 176.2), and other areas with significant bodies of wa-ter. Like woodchucks and rabbits, muskrats are primarily vegetarians. Their special features fit them for an aquatic environment. The most no-ticeable is a narrow, scaly tail – which is also the field mark that best dis-tinguishes them from otters and beavers. Though sometimes found in the

43. Cottontail rabbits are common in most Parkway recreation areas
but are often overlooked because of their tendency to remain motionless
when danger threatens.

Parkway's lakes and rivers, in general the muskrat is not commonly associated with the mountains.

Several middle-sized mammals found along the Parkway are designed for roles as predators. All have a sharp sense of smell, quickness, and the teeth necessary for a meat-eating existence. Beyond these similarities, though, even the two southern Appalachian foxes have adaptations that are unique.

The red fox and the gray fox can both be seen as you travel the Parkway. They would seem to be very similar animals: they are about the same size, and both have large ears, thick tails, pointed snouts, and a generally rusty color. Both hunt mice, rabbits, and birds but also eat fruits and insects. It is true that the tail of the red fox is tipped with white, while that of the gray fox ends in black; however, the more substantial differences are those of life-style rather than appearance. The gray fox is the fox of the forest, where it roams almost exclusively at night. If chased or threatened, it may escape by climbing a tree. The red fox, in contrast, prefers a mixture of fields and woods; it cannot climb but rather runs from danger.

Because most of the Blue Ridge Parkway passes through unbroken forest, the gray fox is more common here than its cousin. Red fox are most likely to occur where fields and pastures are most prevalent – generally from the Roanoke area (about M.P. 110) to the Grandfather Mountain vicinity (M.P. 306).

The mink, another predator, is generally associated with mountain streams. This member of the weasel family patrols along watercourses, its long, slender form allowing it to dodge in and out of tree roots and rocks in search of frogs, salamanders, crayfish, mice, and whatever else is small enough for it to overpower. It also swims well. Mink – 18 to 24 inches long – are larger than the other Blue Ridge weasels and can also be identified by the white chin that interrupts their otherwise solid brown coloration. Mink are probably not common anywhere along the Parkway.

Visitors are much more likely to encounter one of the "go-anywhere, eat-anything" opportunists of the mountains: the raccoon, the opossum, or the skunk. These animals are familiar to most people. Partly because their food requirements are so similar to ours, all of them have adjusted well to human encroachment on their habitats; they are found not only in the mountains but in rural and even urban settings. This ability to live with humans is an adaptation in itself, but each of the three has other special traits.

The raccoon's diet is as varied as that of the bear. (Partly for this reason, raccoons can cause the same sort of campground problems that some bears are known for: rummaging through campers' unstored food.) Raccoons have good sight, hearing, and sense of smell; however, their dinners often depend upon exquisitely sensitive and dexterous paws. A raccoon, rolling over rocks and logs in search of crayfish, salamanders, and aquatic insects, may not even appear to be paying attention to its task. But its sense of touch is quick to recognize prey, and as a result raccoons are very able fishermen. Like many other Blue Ridge mammals, raccoons are primarily nocturnal and not frequently seen. However, a diligent search of sand and mud along any mountain stream, a favorite hunting place for the animal, may well turn up the raccoon's long-fingered tracks, evidence of a recent visit.

The opossum is unlike other Blue Ridge residents in ways too numerous to mention. Its pouch for protecting and raising young, its well-known penchant for playing dead when threatened, and its prehensile tail are all adaptations shared by no other mammal in North America. These traits have helped the possum not only survive but prosper, despite the fact that it is slow afoot and slow-witted as well. Probably its most useful adaptation is its prolific reproductive capacity. While the female raccoon bears three to six young each year, the female opossum produces two litters of six to nine babies each in the same period of time. Many opossums fall prey to foxes, owls, dogs, and automobiles, but their general success is substantiated by the fact that their range has spread northward through the United States in recent years. They seem to be less common on the mountaintops than at lower elevations, probably because in hollows, valleys, and piedmont they benefit from contact with people.

The skunk's most unique adaptation is well known. (In fact, I have even been asked by visitors from a foreign country where skunks are not found where they could go to smell one!) As important as the skunk's "tear gas" defense is, though, its striking black and white coat is just as important to the animal's survival. Like the rattlesnake's warning buzz, the skunk's distinctive markings serve notice at a distance: leave me alone. Generally, it takes only one experience for a potential predator to learn the significance of this warning coloration. As a result, the skunk

44. Though not as well adapted for winter weather as many other Blue Ridge mammals, the opossum survives in the face of this and other threats because it is so prolific.

does not need to risk battle to prove the potency of its defenses. (Ironically, great horned owls, which seem to be immune to the skunk's odor, actually seek them out. Particularly for a predator with such keen night vision, the skunk's bold coloration must make an easy target indeed.)

Two species are found in the Blue Ridge: the striped skunk and the spotted skunk. Like the raccoon and opossum, they eat almost anything. However, skunks especially use their strong claws and forefeet to dig for insects and insect larvae. The striped skunk (called "polecat" by local people) is the larger and more familiar of the two. The spotted skunk (or "civet cat") is very similar in its habits, but its small size (about two pounds, less than half the weight of its cousin) and more extensive white striping make the two easy to tell apart. Spotted skunks are rarer and are only occasionally seen along the Parkway.

The smallest mammals in the forest are both the most common and the least noticed. The major reason they are common is that each individual can fulfill its needs in a small area; the amount of forest necessary to feed one bear supports hundred of mice, for instance. And the major reason they are little noticed is that they try to be. Small mammals have many enemies and few defenses. The squirrel can climb and the mole can tunnel, but for the most part the smallest animals attempt to survive by escaping detection. Even so, many are eaten by predators. Their commonest features, then, are sharp senses to detect danger and an ability to reproduce in staggering numbers. These abundant creatures, though frequently unnoticed by Parkway visitors, feed many of the more celebrated animals of the forest. That is their primary role in the web of life.

Of the small mammals, perhaps the squirrels are most frequently seen. All of them feed primarily on fruits, seeds, and buds, although most will eat insects or nestling birds occasionally. The gray squirrel, a resident of deciduous forests, is the most common squirrel found in the Blue Ridge. Particularly prevalent where oak and hickory abound, gray squirrels spend early morning and late afternoon hours foraging for food. They can be seen then, or heard rustling through leaves or chattering in response to the visitor's invasion. The gray squirrel's larger and darker cousin, the fox squirrel, may very occasionally be found along the Parkway, generally at the lowest elevations.

The uppermost slopes and ridges of the mountains, particularly those dominated by evergreens, are the domain of the lively red squirrel

45. The red squirrel inhabits the higher elevations of the southern Appalachians. When surprised on the ground, it often dashes to the safety of a nearby tree and noisily scolds the intruder.

or "mountain boomer", a small, rusty-brown squirrel with white undersides. As with so many other species, the similarity of the high elevations to northern habitats allows this essentially northern mammal to live as far south as the mountains of northern Georgia. The red squirrel thrives in areas like Grandfather Mountain (M.P. 303), Mount Mitchell State Park (M.P. 355.3), Mount Pisgah (M.P. 408.6), and Richland Balsam (M.P. 431.4), feeding on spruce and fir seeds, mushrooms, and other items. Frequently the red squirrel will aggressively exclude its larger relative, the gray squirrel, where the two meet, but in some areas (like Cone-Price Park, M.P. 295) both animals can be found.

The significance of the cool ridgetop climate is also evident in the distribution of flying squirrels. Throughout the Southeast and most of the mountains, the southern flying squirrel rules the treetops at night, taking over the daytime role of the gray squirrel. At the highest elevations, though, the browner and slightly larger northern flying squirrel is found. Except in the Appalachians, it is not otherwise present south of Pennsylvania. Flying squirrels do not actually fly; rather, large folds of skin connecting their fore and hind legs stretch taut and allow them to glide from tree to tree. They also have large, highly sensitive eyes, which adapt them for an exclusively nocturnal life. Flying squirrels are rarely seen, but the visitor who listens quietly in the woods at night can often detect their birdlike chirping. I was once startled to hear one end its long glide through the trees with a scratching, scrambling landing on a nearby trunk.

Chipmunks are fairly common all along the Parkway, and visitors who have spent much time anywhere in the southern Appalachian woods are familiar with them. Like most of the small mammals, they have many predators, and frequently the presence of a chipmunk is first signaled by the sound of the warning cluck the animal utters whenever it is surprised by an intruder. Still, in some places along the Parkway, chipmunks may be quite bold in their quest for human food.

There are also meat-eaters among the smallest mammals, hunting their animal food like a miniature echo of the forest's larger predators. Through the same woods where the bobcat pursues the cottontail, weasels chase mice. Another diminutive mammal that is far more common than visitors realize, the weasel has a voracious appetite: it eats not only mice but shrews, chipmunks, small birds, and snakes. The long-tailed weasel, found all along the Parkway, occasionally kills rabbits larger than

46. When darkness sends more familiar squirrels to their nests, the
secretive flying squirrel emerges to search the woods for nuts and insects.

itself. The other variety in residence here is the least weasel, so named because it is only the size of a chipmunk. Least weasels live as far north as the Arctic Circle; in this part of North America they are found only in the mountains.

The honor of being the forest's smallest mammalian predators, though, belongs to the shrews. The largest (the short-tailed shrew, also the most common species) is only mouse-sized, and many of the smaller ones are no larger than a person's little finger and weigh only fractions of an ounce. Because they are so tiny, shrews lose body heat rapidly and must constantly search for food to keep from freezing to death. They hunt along runways under leaf litter on the forest floor, and at night some venture up into trees. Since they have little use for sight, their eyes are almost nonexistent; instead, shrews smell or merely blunder across their prey. Insects, earthworms, and other forms of small animal life constitute the bulk of their diet.

Shrews resemble and are closely related to moles, which are also found in the southern mountains. Moles differ primarily in that their highly modified front feet, like small but powerful shovels, are capable of propelling the mole through soil at a remarkable rate. Moles have other adaptations for a life underground, including a lack of external ears and very thick, short fur—both of which help streamline the animal. Like shrews, moles depend on insects, worms, and other invertebrates for their food.

Moles illustrate well the unusual animal designs produced by evolution, designs that allow organisms to exploit new food sources or to escape predators. Another especially good example is the bat, a small mammal with a whole array of unique adaptations. Most obvious are the wings that make it the only mammal capable of true flight. In addition, bats have the ability to "see" in total darkness by using a natural version of radar or sonar. The animal emits high-pitched shrieks as it flies; the sound waves bounce off objects in the woods and return to the bat's ears, informing it of their locations. So refined is this system (called "echolocation") that bats use it to catch moths fluttering through the dark branches of the Blue Ridge forests.

Though no accurate census of Blue Ridge Parkway bats has ever been done, observations in Great Smoky Mountains National Park, Shenandoah National Park, and other nearby areas make it safe to estimate that eight to ten kinds are found here. The habits of all these bats are similar. After spending daylight hours roosting in a hollow tree, cave, or old building, or under loose tree bark, they take wing around dusk. Bats may frequently be seen over bodies of water before sunlight has completely faded. The lakes at the Peaks of Otter (M.P. 85.9) and Julian Price Park (M.P. 296.7), as well as the river at the Linville Falls campground (M.P. 316.4), are good places to watch for bats.

Of all the mammals we have talked about, none can rival in sheer numbers this final group: the mice and their cousins. In the woods and fields at all elevations, members of the various species (including deer mice, wood rats, voles, jumping mice, and others) scurry in search of food. Most are not particularly choosy, eating seeds, berries, grasses, insects, and other odds and ends. In turn, they are themselves eaten.

Danger from predators comes in an intimidating number of forms. Small rodents must avoid snakes, hawks, owls, and nearly every meat-eating mammal already mentioned in this chapter. Many of the predators, in turn, rely principally on mice for their survival and therefore take great numbers. So life on the small mammal scale is fast-paced: births are frequent, maturity is reached in weeks, many young are produced, and death comes early.

The deer mice and the white-footed mice, both woodland inhabitants and closely related, are the members of this group visitors are most likely to encounter. (The deer mice are more common at the higher elevations.) By day they hide in hollow stumps and tree limbs, in rock crevices and nests of leaves. At night, however, they roam, rustling across the forest floor in search of snails or acorns, or perhaps boldly chewing a hole in the bottom of a bag of potato chips forgetfully left on the campsite picnic table. Yet they are rarely seen—except occasionally on foggy, rainy nights, when the driver with a watchful eye may spot mice dashing across the Parkway through the headlights of his car. They are abundant, though, fortunately for the many other creatures that rely on this group for their survival.

A New Lease on Life

More than 60 years after the last native elk were sighted in the Blue Ridge, it was suggested that they be reintroduced into their old haunts. The year was 1917, during the darkest decades for southern Appalachian mammals. The bison, elk, and mountain lion were long gone. The last

47. Mice are a vital part of the food web in southern Appalachian forests.

wolf had been hunted down in the North Carolina wilds 15 years earlier. Deer were almost nonexistent. The few remaining bear and bobcat clung to the rockiest, most remote summits of the Appalachian range. There was, however, a growing feeling in the United States that at least certain "beneficial" wildlife should be conserved. It was in the spirit of this ideal that the chief forester of the Vanderbilt estate near Asheville, North Carolina, had stocked his woods with white-tailed deer a few years earlier, aiding in their recovery.

The same spirit motivated the reintroduction of the elk. So that year more than 100 of the animals were transported from Yellowstone National Park to various parts of Virginia. Twenty-five were released in the vicinity of the Peaks of Otter (M.P. 85.9). This herd took hold, roaming the hills and forests and sometimes appearing in local fields early in the morning or late in the day. Another group was added in 1935, and at one point the Peaks of Otter boasted nearly 85 elk.

But the vast wilderness of pioneer days was gone. Elk following their predecessors' routes down the mountainside to spend the winter in the warmer, lower elevations ended up in apple orchards instead of virgin timber. There, many were shot by the orchards' owners, who lost hundreds of dollars' worth of apples and trees to the wandering animals. Other elk contracted a brain parasite and died. Perhaps the survivors through the years were weakened by the genetic effects of inbreeding. At any rate, although remnants of the Peaks of Otter herd survived until the early 1970s, the elk finally disappeared once again. There is not enough wild land to support them; no new attempts to establish elk are planned.

The restocking attempt, though, symbolized the slowly changing attitudes and conditions that have improved the status of southern Appalachian wildlife. Deer, bear, wild turkey, and other animals all made a significant comeback during the same span of time. And perhaps the most inspiring story is that of the mountain lion. One summer night in 1978, Park Ranger Warner Williams surprised a large cat in a field along the Parkway. The spotlight clearly showed its eight-foot length, its long tail, its lack of spots. Near Dripping Rock Trail (M.P. 9.6) in the autumn of 1980, Ranger John Howard also saw an animal that fit the description of a mountain lion, a species that "officially" disappeared from the southern Appalachians over 100 years ago.

These are not the only such incidents in National Park Service files:

there have been continual (if sporadic) reports from people who say they have seen the big cat, also known as a puma or "panther." Some have turned out to be false alarms; bobcats, loose hounds, and even deer can be mistaken for mountain lions in bad light or by inexperienced observers. Other reports, however, are difficult to question. Skeptics note that, despite the sightings, no reliable evidence has been produced that mountain lions do exist in the Blue Ridge. (Indeed, the nearest native populations of these animals are in Florida and Canada.) However, the debate remains an open one, and it is entirely possible that an animal once thought extinct here is returning to claim its former home. If so, it is an indication that the preservation of wild lands can make a difference in the survival of wildlife. The national parks of the southern Appalachians play a part in that preservation.

Mountain lions and bears have no more significance in nature than fungi or long-horned timber beetles, yet they are certainly more celebrated. There are naturalists who are privately discouraged by this fact: are too many visitors, they wonder, fascinated by the local mammals but only dimly aware of other aspects of natural history? And will they leave the park with an understanding of *all* the reasons it exists?

Perhaps they will. But many of the important concepts of ecology—the uniqueness of adaptations, the strong control exerted by the environment on plants and animals—can be readily observed in the mammals alone. What better way to start learning nature's story than to begin with the aspects that interest you? It doesn't make a great deal of difference what chapter you scan first; if it is interesting, eventually you read the whole book.

Humans

One mammal deserves a chapter all to itself: the animal you will encounter most frequently on the Parkway, concentrated especially in campgrounds and picnic areas, on hiking trails, and along the roadway itself, in numbers exceeding 16 million a year. It is the human being. Humans are prevalent not only along the Parkway but throughout the southern Appalachians. And of all the thousands of organisms that occur here, they play—*we* play—the single most significant role in the southern Appalachian natural system.

If the human who first set foot in the southern mountains commemorated the event with some kind of marker or monument, it has never been found. From ancient artifacts unearthed at places like the Peaks of Otter (M.P. 85.9), however, archaeologists have established that the southern Appalachians have been inhabited for thousands of years. The earliest peoples to live here led simple lives. They hunted native deer, bear, buffalo, and other animals; gathered nuts, berries, and roots; and wandered about in pursuit of plenty. Many spent summers in the cool higher elevations, then migrated to warmer valleys and coves when the snows of winter began to fall.

Whatever larger migrations occurred, whatever ebbings and flowings of races and strains and tribes washed through the southern Appalachians, are still largely a puzzle. Most of what we do know about the primitive peoples of this region is relatively recent history—it comes from the letters and journals of the first Europeans here, the traders and adventurers who first ventured beyond the barrier of the Blue Ridge.

In the late seventeenth and early eighteenth centuries, several tribes of native Americans inhabited the areas now traversed by the Blue Ridge Parkway. By far the largest and most significant group were the Cherokees, who populated a broad area stretching from the vicinity of present-day Asheville, North Carolina, into the Smokies of eastern Tennessee. The earliest white explorers found no more than 20,000 or 30,000 of them, thinly dispersed throughout the region.

The native American peoples had an impact on the natural environment they lived in, but not a great one. The subtlety of their influence was due not only to their modest numbers but also to their modest life-style. The Cherokees lived in towns and villages; they grew corn, pota-toes, beans, and other crops in the area's rich river-bottom soils. Like the prehistoric peoples before them, they also relied to a great extent on the products of the forest. The wilderness had plenty to give and easily ac-commodated the demands humans placed upon it.

Beginning in the mid-1700s, though, new humans appeared on the scene—people who began to make new demands and have new kinds of impact. This period marked the beginning of European settlement in the southern Appalachians.

The mountains' first European homesteaders arrived well before the American Revolution. They found here a marvelous, rich land. There were trees in the forests that five men together couldn't throw their arms around, and passenger pigeons that would throng past in flocks that dark-ened the sky for 15 minutes at a time. There were also the dangers and hardships of any wilderness. The settlers set to the task of surviving.

Initially, their numbers were small. Eager to test their mettle against a vast, rugged wilderness, or to escape religious prejudice and taxes, a hardy few moved with ax and rifle into the southern Appalachians. Some struggled over the steep Blue Ridge escarpment into the North Carolina backcountry. Others marched down the Shenandoah Valley from Pennsyl-vania, following a centuries-old Indian war trail into Virginia. Wherever these pioneers settled, their life-styles became of necessity much like those of the native Americans who already lived in the region: they gath-ered whatever they could find, killed whatever they could hit, and raised whatever would grow.

The earliest European settlers probably had little more impact on the natural communities of the mountains than their predecessors did—but that soon changed. After the French and Indian War ended in 1763, there was a surge of people into the region. Germans and Scotch-Irish who had landed in Pennsylvania found that all the land there was either already populated or too expensive to buy, so they turned south. Hun-dreds trundled down the same Indian trail that earlier pioneers had used (now somewhat grandiosely renamed "the Great Philadelphia Wagon

Road"). They built their cabins on the best land they could find. As the valleys grew progressively more settled and more expensive, settlers moved up into the coves and hollows of higher elevations.

The impact of humans on the mountains soon increased substantially. Most significantly, the region now had more mouths to feed, and—in the "Kentucky long rifle"—a devastatingly efficient tool to use in feeding them. The large game species, as has already been mentioned, rapidly disappeared. So, too, did those animals that competed with man: the turkeys that damaged cornfields; the raccoons, weasels, and foxes that raided chicken houses; the wolves and bears that killed hogs and sheep.

In addition, the act of clearing and farming land changed the natural communities. Not only was forest habitat destroyed, but wherever slopes were plowed, the rains soon washed the topsoil away. It took only a few years of cultivation to ruin such fields, turning them eventually into poor pasture or poorer second-growth forest.

Decades of increasing human influence passed. By the late 1800s

48. Later settlers in the southern Appalachians homesteaded the hills at high elevations. Some of their original cabins still exist along the Parkway.

49. Clearing steep lands eventually led to serious erosion problems. This photograph, taken in 1936, shows the head of Basin Creek at Doughton Park.

many formerly abundant animals were either extinct in the area or nearly so. The proud Cherokee and other tribes had long since been decimated and scattered. Tons of soil had washed from southern Appalachian slopes down southern Appalachian creeks. In the process, forest nutrients that had built up for centuries were lost—muddy water over the dam.

About the turn of the century, commercial lumbering interests moved into the mountains in earnest. The more readily accessible trees of flat-land forests had already been cut, but plenty of timber remained on the rugged heights of the southern Appalachians. Axes, saws, and logging railroads extended the influence of man to the mountains' very summits.

Of all the changes that humans had wrought in the mountains, none had an impact to equal that of logging. An estimated 750,000 acres of spruce-fir forest existed on the southern Appalachian summits at the time of the Civil War. Today, after logging, only 60,000 acres remain. And worse than the actual cutting of timber was the damage caused by the fires that followed. Leftover limbs and branches, remaining on the ground after the logs had been hauled away, often ignited into sprawling infernos. The destruction these fires did to mountain soils is incalculable. (Along the Parkway, the best example of a former burned-over area can be found at Graveyard Fields, M.P. 418.8.)

In addition, the conspicuous changes in the mountains have been at-tended by less visible ones. When the spruce-fir forests were destroyed, for instance, other things suffered with them. Several varieties of lichen that grow only on southern Appalachian spruces and firs have been brought to the edge of extinction. On Mount Mitchell (M.P. 355.3), log-ging done near the turn of the century eliminated the black-capped chicka-dee from the mountain's summit. The trees have grown back, but the bird as yet has not returned.

I could list a number of other changes humans have brought to the southern Appalachians. Some of the effects of our accidental introduc-tions of foreign plants and animals here are dealt with in other chapters. So are the possible connections between man and the formation and maintenance of balds. Dozen of other examples could be mentioned.

But perhaps the list is long enough already. The point is made: hu-mans have affected the mountains. This is no longer wilderness.

There is a little more to the story, however. For as surely as these southern mountains have molded the plant and animal communities that

50. Though the valuable trees on flatter lands were cut decades earlier, large-scale logging in the mountains did not begin until the turn of the century. Special steam engines were developed to handle the mountains' steep grades.

ride their backs, so too has their massive influence touched man. For decades of American history, the towering Appalachians blocked the way west. When finally the tide of migration could be contained no longer, it burst around the mountains rather than through them. Settlement progressed north of the mountains by moving across Pennsylvania to Pittsburgh, then down the Ohio River Valley. South of the mountains it traveled westward across the flatter Gulf Coast lands.

In the southern Appalachians themselves, where the mountains made travel virtually impossible, civilization by comparison infiltrated at a snail's pace. As late as 1905, a government agent reported that "the population is sparse, and the roads wretched."[1] But beyond the physical problems, says another writer, potential settlers were intimidated by the mere existence of "an unbroken, unlimited, unknown, and mysterious wilderness."[2]

To be sure, man eventually began to overcome this forbidding land. Once new towns were erected, roads gradually improved, railroads constructed, and trees cut, the process of dismembering the wilderness was well under way.

But by the early part of this century, a newborn ethic of conservation had begun to overtake the unchecked forces of development. The public-at-large was beginning to realize what certain farsighted individuals had seen for some time: the wild, unspoiled lands of the United States were fast disappearing, and if any were to be saved, action needed to be immediate. During the late 1800s and early 1900s, many thousands of acres of western lands were set aside as national parks, and shortly thereafter, sentiment swelled for the creation of national parks in the East. When the nation's eyes surveyed the eastern landscape, they saw one area where human encroachment had been stalled, one area that—despite the undeniable presence of man's influence—still had stands of virgin timber, and tangles where the bear and bobcat yet held sway. This was the southern Appalachians.

Congress eventually authorized two national parks in the southern Appalachian region. Since many of the lands to be included in them

---

1. H.B. Ayers and W.W. Ashe, "The Southern Appalachian Forests," United States Geological Survey Forestry Series, Professional Paper 31 (1905), 25.
2. Hugh Talmage Lefler and Albert Ray Newsome, *North Carolina: The History of a Southern State* (Chapel Hill: Univ. of North Carolina Press, 1954), 20.

were under private ownership, there were some delays before the parks became "official." Nonetheless, on July 3, 1936, President Franklin D. Roosevelt dedicated the first of them: Shenandoah National Park in Virginia. Four years later he presided over similar ceremonies at Great Smoky Mountains National Park, which straddles the Tennessee–North Carolina border. During the same period, large expanses of timbered land were set aside as national forests, adding to the protection of natural areas in the southern Appalachians.

Meanwhile, the proposal had been advanced that the nation take further advantage of the unspoiled southern mountains by building a scenic parkway through them, to stretch from Shenandoah National Park in the north to Great Smoky Mountains National Park in the south. This parkway, it was suggested, could allow visitors to experience the full flavor of the region's culture and its natural history.

So the Blue Ridge Parkway came into being. In September 1935 the first shovelful of earth was turned in its construction. Except for a short unfinished section around Grandfather Mountain (M.P. 299.5 to M.P. 304.9), where traffic is routed to a nearby federal highway, the Parkway stretches 469 miles through the heart of the largest expanse of wild land in the eastern United States.

The mountains created this wild land. They are responsible for growing its diverse forests, for nurturing its wide array of salamanders, for guiding its hawks south during the cooling days of autumn. Throughout the preceding chapters I have tried continually to stress this point, for it is the heart, the very essence, of the Blue Ridge Parkway's natural history story. The mountains have made this a special place.

Moreover, the mountains slowed the onslaught of human civilization until the time arrived when people came to *comprehend* that this is a special place. The mountains, in other words, not only created a unique natural world – they helped preserve it.

They preserved it long enough for us to realize that they could not preserve it forever. Had national park and national forest lands not been set aside when they were, irreparable damage would undoubtedly have been done to the remaining southern Appalachian natural communities.

51. An emerging conservation ethic during the early decades of the twentieth century led to the preservation and restoration of much southern Appalachian land.

52. American visitors to the Blue Ridge Parkway can appreciate both its beauty and the fact that they are its owners.

But that damage was avoided, and today's Blue Ridge Parkway visitor can see and explore thousands of acres of wild lands, largely unchanged from the way they were centuries ago.

We must always be mindful of the fact, though, that these lands continue to need our concerned stewardship. Humans, for better or for worse, will continue to play a role in the natural environment here. A vigilant regard for the preservation of the southern Appalachians should be an inseparable part of that role.

Appendix

This appendix includes checklists for the ferns, wildflowers, trees, fish, amphibians, reptiles, birds, and mammals found along the Blue Ridge Parkway. It will give the Parkway visitor an idea of what plants and animals he may encounter as he visits the various recreation areas along the 469-mile road.

Let me make several comments about the lists.

First, I have covered only four or five Parkway recreation areas in each checklist. Because the Parkway's flora and fauna vary only a little from place to place, I have chosen representative locations in the interest of simplicity.

Second, I would like to give credit to the many agencies, groups, and individuals who provided information and observations for the checklists. Limited space requires me to leave many names unmentioned, but each has contributed to our knowledge of the Blue Ridge Parkway and the southern Appalachians.

Yet despite all the work that has been done, much about the Parkway's natural history remains unknown or at least unrecorded. Should you observe a plant or animal not noted on the checklists, please report it to Blue Ridge Parkway personnel. In that way you will be making your own contribution to our knowledge of the southern Appalachian environment.

With the exception of the seasonally arranged wildflower bloom calendar, the lists are arranged taxonomically. Both the common and scientific names of the organisms are provided. An "X" after the plant or animal's name indicates that it has been found in the vicinity of the listed recreation area, "E" that it has not been recorded for the area but should be expected, and "?" that it might be present.

Ferns and Fern Allies

In some recreation areas (like Rocky Knob), the ferns have been extensively inventoried and are well known; in others, little field work has been done. The information in this list has been generously provided by Professor J. Dan Pittillo of Western Carolina University, and Randall Kendrick, Robyn Nolen, and others of the National Park Service staff.

Species	Peaks of Otter	Rocky Knob	Cone-Price	Crabtree Meadows	Craggy Gardens
Fir or cliff clubmoss (*Lycopodium selago*)					X
Shining clubmoss (*L. lucidulum*)	X	X	X		X
Running clubmoss (*L. clavatum*)		X	X		X
Tree clubmoss (*L. obscurum*)		X	X		X
Ground cedar (*L. tristachyum*)	X	X		X	
Ground-pine (*L. complanatum*)	X	X			X
Grape fern (*Botrychium dissectum*)	X	X			
Rattlesnake fern (*B. virginianum*)	X	X		X	
Royal fern (*Osmunda regalis*)	X	X	X		
Interrupted fern (*O. claytoniana*)	X	X	X	X	
Cinnamon fern (*O. cinnamonea*)	X	X	X	X	X
Hartford or climbing fern (*Lygodium palmatum*)				X	
Large woodsia (*Woodsia obtusa*)		X			
Fragile fern (*Cystopteris fragilis*)	X	X		X	
Bulblet fern (*C. bulbifera*)				X	
Sensitive fern (*Onoclea sensibilis*)	X	X			
Marsh fern (*Dryopteris Thelypteris*)		X			
New York fern (*D. noveboracensis*)	X	X	X	X	X
Long beech fern (*D. Phegopteris*)				X	
Broad beech fern (*D. hexagonoptera*)	X	X		X	
Spinulose wood fern (*D. spinulosa*)		X		X	
Fancy fern (*D. intermedia*)		X			
Crested wood fern (*D. cristata*)			X	X	
Oak fern (*D. disjuncta*)	X				
Marginal shield fern (*D. marginalis*)	X	X		X	
Christmas fern (*Polystichum acrostichoides*)	X	X	X	X	X
Hay-scented fern (*Dennstaedtia punctilobula*)	X	X	X	X	X
Silvery spleenwort (*Athyrium thelypterioides*)	X	X			X
Lady fern (*A. filix-femina*)	X	X	X	X	X
Glade fern (*A. pycnocarpon*)		X			
Walking fern (*Camptosorus rhizophyllus*)		X			
Mountain spleenwort (*Asplenium montanum*)		X			X
Blackstem spleenwort (*A. resiliens*)		X			
Maidenhair spleenwort (*A. trichomanes*)		X			
Ebony spleenwort (*A. platyneuron*)	X	X	X	X	
Common chainfern (*Woodwardia areolata*)		X			
Purple cliffbrake (*Pellaea atropurpurea*)	X				
Maidenhair fern (*Adiantum pedatum*)	X	X		X	
Bracken (*Pteridium aquilinum*)	X	X	X	X	
Common polypody (*Polypodium virginianum*)	X	X	X	X	X
Resurrection fern (*P. polypodioides*)					X

Appendix

Wildflowers: A Bloom Calendar for the Parkway

This list includes only the Blue Ridge Parkway's showier flowers, arranged roughly in the order in which they bloom throughout the year. Weather plays a big role in determining when flowers emerge, so the peak bloom times given are necessarily approximations. The dates for the Virginia section of the Parkway are typically earlier than those along the North Carolina section because of Virginia's lower elevations. Wildflower concentrations are listed by milepost. The letters "PA" represent picnic areas. This information is reproduced by courtesy of the National Park Service, Blue Ridge Parkway.

Flower	Peak Bloom	Location (by Milepost)
Skunk cabbage (*Symplocarpus foetidus*)	Feb.–Mar.	145.5, 159.8–160.5, 176.1, 185.8, 217, 251.5, 270–271
Dandelion (*Taraxacum officinale*)	Feb.–June	Common along roadside
Dwarf iris (*Iris verna*)	Mar.–Apr.	196, 260.5, 303.4
Spring beauty (*Claytonia* spp.)	Mar.–May	294, 367.6 PA, 433.4
May apple (*Podophyllum peltatum*)	Mar.–Apr.	1.5–2.1, 5.3–5.7, 74–76.4, 196.9, 216.5, 266, 296–297, 315–317, 320.8, 339.5
Serviceberry (*Amelanchier arborea*)	Mar.–May	23–23.6, 91–100, 169.8–169.9, 241–242, 294–297, 308.3, 368–378
Silverbell tree (*Halesia carolina*)	Mar.–May	344.1–355.3, 461–469
Birdfoot violet (*Viola pedata*)	Mar.–May	85.8, 147.4, 202, 260.5, 379
Buttercup (*Ranunculus* spp.)	Mar.–June	Common along roadside
Wild strawberry (*Fragaria virginiana*)	Mar.–June	Common along roadside
Crested dwarf iris (*Iris cristata*)	Apr.–May	85–86, 195, 198, 210, 217, 250.8, 273.4, 295–298, 339.5, 379
Squirrel corn (*Dicentra canadensis*)	Apr.–May	367.6 PA, 458.2–Heintooga Spur Rd.
Tuliptree (*Liriodendron tulipifera*)	Apr.–May	Common in low woods and coves
Indian paintbrush (*Castilleja coccinea*)	Apr.–May	163–164, 369–371
Great chickweed (*Stellaria pubera*)	Apr.–May	Common in rich, moist woods
Solomon's seal (*Polygonatum biflorum*)	Apr.–May	Common on moist wooded slopes and coves
Phacelia (*Phacelia* spp.)	Apr.–May	297, 370–375

Flower	Peak Bloom	Location (by Milepost)
Bloodroot (*Sanguinaria canadensis*)	Apr.–May	11–12.4, 32, 49, 85.6, 139.5, 176.1, 191–193, 294, 375–376
Princess tree (*Paulownia tomentosa*)	Apr.–May	63.6, 97, 100–123, 381–382, 396, 400
Golden groundsel (*Senecio aureus*)	Apr.–May	29.1, 85.8 PA, 330–340
Pinxter-flower (*Rhododendron nudiflorum*)	Apr.–May	4, 53.6, 69.7, 76–81, 92–97, 138.6, 145.5, 154.5 PA, 162.9, 211.6, 217–222, 350–351, 412–423
Heal-all (*Prunella vulgaris*)	Apr.–frost	Common along roadside
Wake-robin (*Trillium* spp.)	Apr.–May	175, 200–216, 339–340, 364.6
Fetterbush (*Leucothoe racemosa*)	late Apr.–May	241.1, 379
Redbud tree (*Cercis canadensis*)	late Apr.–May	40.2, 47–51, 54, 59.8–60, 61.4–68, 102–105, 124.7–124.9
Dutchman's-breeches (*Dicentra cucullaria*)	Apr.–June	32.3, 36.4, 83–85, 167, 367.6 PA, 433.2, 441.2, 458.2–Heintooga Spur Rd.
Foamflower (*Tiarella cordifolia*)	Apr.–June	83–86, 167, 296–297, 339.5, 367.7 PA
False Solomon's seal (*Smilacina racemosa*)	Apr.–June	Common along roadside
Black locust (*Robinia pseudo-acacia*)	Apr.–June	100–123, 167–169, 199–201, 209, 367–368, 383
Witch-hobble or hobblebush (*Viburnum alnifolium*)	Apr.–June	Higher elevations in rich, moist woods
Carolina rhododendron (*Rhododendron minus*)	late Apr.–June	308–310, 404–411
Flowering dogwood (*Cornus florida*)	May	0–6, 16–19, 36.2–39.1, 46–48, 63.3–64.2, 85.8 PA, 105–107, 140–142, 194–196, 200–202, 217–219, 230–232, 344, 378–382
Large-flowered trillium (*Trillium grandiflorum*)	May	3–7, 33.7, 64–85, 154.5 PA, 167–169, 175, 330–340, 370–375
Fraser magnolia (*Magnolia fraseri*)	May	173–174, 181–185, 200, 252–253, 291, 294.7, 317.3, 339.3

Appendix

Flower	Peak Bloom	Location (by Milepost)
Bluet (*Houstonia* spp.)	Apr.–June	83–86, 200.2, 243, 355–368
Field hawkweed or king devil (*Hieracium pratense*)	May–June	Frequent in open bays and fields
Wild geranium (*Geranium maculatum*)	May–June	84–86, 170–172, 199, 211.6, 297.2, 375
Hawthorn (*Crataegus* spp.)	May–June	155–176, 365.6, 368
Small's groundsel (*Senecio smallii*)	May–June	29.1, 85.8 PA, 330–340
Bristly locust (*Robinia hispida*)	May–June	85–86, 167–174, 308.3, 347.9, 350.1, 422.1
Pinkshell (*Rhododendron vaseyi*)	May–June	305.2, 342–343, 349–351, 419–426, 440–451
Red-berried elder (*Sambucus pubens*)	May–June	Higher elevations in rich, moist woods
Flame azalea (*Rhododendron calendulaceum*)	early May –June	138.6, 144–145, 149.5, 164–166, 195.9, 217–221, 308–310, 368–380, 412–423
Fire pink (*Silene virginica*)	May–June	1–2, 60.7, 69.7, 85.8 PA, 154.5 PA, 168, 176, 241 PA, 339.3 PA, 367–375, 393.6, 404–408
Allegheny blackberry (*Rubus* spp.)	May–July	6, 167.2, 239.9, 305–315, 339.5, 367.6 PA
Staghorn sumac (*Rhus typhina*)	May–June	Common along roadside in dry, rocky areas
Bowman's-root (*Gillenia trifoliata*)	May–June	24–45, 89–93, 149.5, 175–176, 260, 272, 332, 368–369
Bead lily (*Clintonia umbellulata*)	May–June	Common in rich, moist deciduous woods
New Jersey tea (*Ceanothus americanus*)	May–June	42–43, 91–100, 138.4, 197, 211, 241, 328.6
Bittersweet (*Celastrus orbiculatus*)	May–June Aug.–Sept. (berry)	242.4, 383, 394, 396
Galax (*Galax aphylla*)	May–July	Common in deciduous forests, open rocky areas
Fly-poison (*Amianthium muscaetoxicum*)	May–July	210–216, 294, 406–408
Phlox (*Phlox carolina*)	May–July	4, 79–82, 91–101, 163–164, 197, 200–202, 219–221, 248 PA, 339.3 PA, 370–380, 409–413, 421–435

Flower	Peak Bloom	Location (by Milepost)
Columbine (*Aquilegia canadensis*)	May–July	83–85, 74–75, 168, 197, 339.3 PA, 370–378, 409.6
Bladder campion (*Silene cucubalus*)	May–Aug.	350, 376–381
Queen Anne's lace (*Daucus carota*)	May–Sept.	Common along road-sides and in open fields
Virginia spiderwort (*Tradescantia subaspera*)	late May–July	85.8, 191.6, 197, 380–381
Mountain laurel (*Kalmia latifolia*)	late May–June	130.5, 162.9, 167, 184–186, 347.9, 379.0, 380, 398.4–398.5, 400, 402–410, 419
Catawba rhododendron (*Rhododendron catawbiense*)	June	44.9, 77–83, 130.5, 138.6, 233, 239, 247, 266.8, 305.1, 308.3, 348–350, 364.1, 367.7, 407–408, 418–419, 421–425, 431, 451.2
Viper's bugloss (*Echium vulgare*)	June	5–40, 85–93
Sundrop (*Oenothera fruiticosa*)	June	8–10, 89–91, 194, 200–210, 229, 237, 270.6, 351–352, 355–360, 370–375
Tree of heaven (*Ailanthus altissima*)	June July–Oct. (fruit)	Common along road-sides in Virginia
Goat's-beard (*Aruncus dioicus*)	June	10–11, 24, 85–89, 176.7, 240, 337.6, 370–375
Butterfly weed (*Asclepias tuberosa*)	June–Aug.	Common on roadbanks
Beardtongue (*Penstemon* spp.)	June–July	44.4, 89–91, 97–102, 154.5 PA, 254.5, 339–340, 370–372
American elder (*Sambucus canadensis*)	June–July	29, 75–81, 85.8 PA, 136–138, 272–275, 311.2
Fragrant thimbleberry (*Rubus odoratus*)	June–July	18, 74.7, 82–86, 339.3 PA, 369–372, 406–408
Rosebay rhododendron (*Rhododendron maximum*)	June–July	144–145, 162.9, 169 PA, 186–188, 190, 193, 202, 210, 232–233, 339.3 PA, 352–353, 455–456
Sourwood (*Oxydendrum arboreum*)	June–July	80–86, 96–97, 102–106, 231–232, 242.5, 321–327, 375–380

Appendix

Flower	Peak Bloom	Location (by Milepost)
Mountain ash (*Sorbus americana*)	June–July Sept.–Oct. (berry)	Higher elevations: spruce-fir forest, Peaks of Otter, Doughton Park, Mt. Mitchell, Mt. Pisgah
False hellebore (*Veratrum viride*)	June–Aug.	83–89, 174, 200, 364.6, 400
Deptford pink (*Dianthus armeria*)	June–Aug.	Common along grassy roadsides
Coreopsis (*Coreopsis pubescens*)	June–Aug.	29.6, 77, 87–102, 157, 190, 207.8, 306
Butter and eggs (*Linaria vulgaris*)	June–Aug.	Locally abundant along roadsides and waste places
Turk's-cap lily (*Lilium superbum*)	June–Aug.	74–79, 167–169, 187.6, 287, 364–368, 406–411
Mullein (*Verbascum thapsus*)	June–Sept.	Common along road-sides on dry banks
Bull thistle (*Carduus lanceolatus*)	late June–frost	Common along road-sides and in pastures at lower elevations
Black cohosh (*Cimicifuga racemosa*)	July	6, 85.8 PA, 169 PA, 374
Tall meadow-rue (*Thalictrum polygamum*)	July	85.8 PA, 155.2, 248
Fleabane (*Erigeron strigosus*)	July	Common along road-sides and in fields
Ox-eye daisy (*Chrysanthemum leucanthemum*)	July	Common along road-sides and in fields
Yarrow (*Achillea millefolium*)	July	Common along road-sides and in fields
Black-eyed Susan (*Rudbeckia hirta*)	July	Common along road-sides and in fields
Milkweed (*Asclepias syriaca*)	July–Aug.	85–86, 167–176
Bergamot (*Monarda fistulosa*)	July–Aug.	38.8, 85–89, 368–374
Tall coneflower (*Rudbeckia laciniata*)	July–Aug.	36, 74–79, 161.2, 228.1, 314, 359–368, 423, 432, 435
Oswego-tea (*Monarda didyma*)	July–Aug.	Common at higher ele-vations in wet areas
Starry campion (*Silene stellata*)	July–Sept.	85–86, 378–380
Bellflower (*Campanula americana*)	July–Sept.	74–83, 370–375
White snakeroot (*Eupatorium rugosum*)	July–Oct.	Common along roadsides
Jewelweed (*Impatiens capensis*)	Aug.	Common along road-sides in wet areas
Boneset (*Eupatorium perfoliatum*)	Aug.	29.1, 85.8 PA, 151, 167, 247, 314, 365.6

Flower	Peak Bloom	Location (by Milepost)
Ironweed (*Veronia noveboracensis*)	Aug.	85.8 PA, 186, 209, 245, 248
Joe-Pye weed (*Eupatorium purpureum*)	Aug.	6, 85.8 PA, 146, 186, 209, 248, 339.3 PA, 357–359
Pokeberry (*Phytolacca americana*)	Aug.	6, 74.7, 151, 239.9, 323, 376.9
Cardinal-flower (*Lobelia cardinalis*)	Aug.	Wet areas, infrequent
Virgin's-bower (*Clematis virginiana*)	Aug.	13.1, 85.8, 176.1, 216, 285–289, 313–314
Blazing-star (*Liatris spicata*)	Aug.–Sept.	75–76, 101, 241.9, 305.1, 369–370
Sneezeweed (*Helenium autumnale*)	Aug.–Sept.	29.1, 176.1, 209.6, 229, 313–314
Angelica (*Angelica triquinata*)	Aug.–Sept.	294.7, 339.5, 355, 364.1, 418–419, 451.2
Nodding ladies'-tresses (*Spiranthes cernua*)	Aug.–frost	365–368
Gentian (*Gentiana* spp.)	late Aug.–frost	85.8, 363–368
Goldenrod (*Solidago* spp.)	Sept.	Common along roadsides and in fields
Aster (*Aster* spp.)	Sept.	Common along roadsides and in fields
Wingstem (*Actinomeris alternifolia*)	Aug.–Oct.	6, 85–86, 88, 154.4, 271.9, 330.8
Witch-hazel (*Hamamelis virginiana*)	late Sept.–Oct.	130.5, 293.3, 295.4, 305.1, 308.3, 339.5, 347.6, 367.7

Trees

This information is drawn from *Important Plant Habitats of the Blue Ridge Parkway* by J. Dan Pittillo and Thomas E. Govus (National Park Service Report, 1978), and from National Park Service records, and has been greatly supplemented by many Blue Ridge Parkway field personnel. In the interest of brevity I have (somewhat arbitrarily) excluded shrubs from this list. Nomenclature generally follows M.L. Fernald, *Gray's Manual of Botany*, 8th ed. (New York: Van Nostrand, 1950).

Species	Otter Cr.-James R.	Peaks of Otter	Rocky Knob	Cone-Price	Linville Falls
Fraser fir (*Abies fraseri*)				X	
Eastern hemlock (*Tsuga canadensis*)	X	X	X	X	X
Carolina hemlock (*T. caroliniana*)		X	X	X	X
Red spruce (*Picea rubens*)				X	
Eastern white pine (*Pinus strobus*)	X	X	X	X	X
Shortleaf pine (*P. echinata*)	X				
Virginia pine (*P. virginiana*)	X	X	X		X
Pitch pine (*P. rigida*)	X	X	X		X
Table Mountain pine (*P. pungens*)	X	X	X	X	X
Common juniper (*Juniperus communis*)			X		
Eastern red cedar (*J. virginiana*)	X	X	X		
Silky willow (*Salix sericea*)		X		X	X
Large-toothed aspen (*Populus grandidentata*)		X			
Butternut (*Juglans cinerea*)	X		X	X	X
Black walnut (*J. nigra*)	X	X	X	X	X
Bitternut hickory (*Carya cordiformis*)	X	X	X	X	X
Shagbark hickory (*C. ovata*)	X	X	X	X	X
Mockernut hickory (*C. tomentosa*)	X	X	X	X	X
Pignut hickory (*C. glabra*)	X	X	X	X	X
Hazelnut (*Corylus americana*)	X	X		X	
American hop hornbeam (*Ostrya virginiana*)	X	X	X	X	X
Ironwood (*Carpinus caroliniana*)	X	X	X	X	X
Black birch (*Betula lenta*)	X	X	X	X	X
Yellow birch (*B. lutea*)		X	X	X	X
River birch (*B. nigra*)	X				
Common alder (*Alnus serrulata*)		X	X		
American beech (*Fagus grandifolia*)	X	X	X	X	X
Chinese chestnut (*Castanea molissima*)			X		
American chestnut—sprouts (*C. dentata*)	X	X	X	X	X
Chinquapin (*C. pumila*)	X	X			X
White oak (*Quercus alba*)	X	X	X	X	X
Chestnut oak (*Q. prinus*)	X	X	X	X	X
Northern red oak (*Q. rubra*)	X	X	X	X	X
Black oak (*Q. velutina*)	X	X	X	X	X
Scarlet oak (*Q. coccinea*)	X	X	X	X	X
Black Jack oak (*Q. marilandica*)		X	X		
Scrub oak (*Q. ilicifolia*)		X			X
Spanish oak (*Q. falcata*)			X		
Slippery elm (*Ulmus rubra*)	X	X	X		X
American elm (*U. americana*)	X		X		X

Species	Otter Cr.–James R.	Peaks of Otter	Rocky Knob	Cone-Price	Linville Falls
Cucumbertree (*Magnolia acuminata*)		X	X	X	X
Fraser magnolia (*M. fraseri*)			X	X	X
Tuliptree (*Liriodendron tulipifera*)	X	X	X	X	X
Pawpaw (*Asimina triloba*)	X	X			
Sassafras (*Sassafras albidum*)	X	X	X	X	X
Witch-hazel (*Hamamelis virginiana*)	X	X	X	X	X
Sweet gum (*Liquidambar Styraciflua*)	X				X
American sycamore (*Platanus occidentalis*)	X	X	X		X
Pear (*Pyrus communis*)	X	X		X	
Apple (*P. malus*)	X	X	X	X	X
Crab apple (*P. angustifolia*)	X		X	X	
Red chokeberry (*P. arbutifolia*)				X	
Mountain ash (*Sorbus americana*)		X		X	
Serviceberry (*Amelanchier laevis*)	X	X	X	X	X
Hawthorn (*Crataegus* spp.)	X	X	X	X	X
Peach (*Prunus persica*)		X			
Fire cherry (*P. pennsylvanica*)	X	X		X	X
Sweet cherry (*P. avium*)			X		
Sour cherry (*P. cerasus*)			X		
Black cherry (*P. serotina*)	X	X	X	X	
Choke cherry (*P. virginiana*)		X		X	X
Redbud (*Cercis canadensis*)	X	X	X		X
Black locust (*Robinia pseudo-acacia*)	X	X	X	X	X
Tree-of-heaven (*Ailanthus altissima*)	X	X			
American holly (*Ilex opaca*)	X		X	X	X
Mountain holly (*I. montana*)		X	X	X	
American bladdernut (*Staphylea trifolia*)	X				
Mountain maple (*Acer spicatum*)		X	X		
Striped maple (*A. pennsylvanicum*)	X	X	X	X	X
Sugar maple (*A. saccharum*)	X	X	X	X	X
Red maple (*A. rubrum*)	X	X	X	X	X
Silver maple (*A. saccharinum*)	X		X	X	
Box elder (*A. negundo*)	X	X	X		
Black maple (*A. nigrum*)		X			
Yellow buckeye (*Aesculus octandra*)				X	X
Basswood (*Tilia americana*)	X	X	X	X	X
White basswood (*T. heterophylla*)					X
Black gum (*Nyssa sylvatica*)	X	X	X	X	X
Hercules'-club (*Aralia spinosa*)					X
Flowering dogwood (*Cornus florida*)	X	X	X	X	X

Species	Otter Cr.– James R.	Peaks of Otter	Rocky Knob	Cone-Price	Linville Falls
Alternate-leaved dogwood (*C. alternifolia*)	X	X	X	X	X
Sourwood (*Oxydendrum arboreum*)	X	X		X	X
Persimmon (*Diospyros virginiana*)	X	X		X	
White ash (*Fraxinus americana*)	X	X	X	X	X
Green ash (*F. pennsylvanica*)	X	X			
Fringe-tree (*Chionanthus virginica*)	X				
Princess-tree (*Paulownia tomentosa*)	X	X			

Fish

This list has been compiled from National Park Service records, along with those supplied by Joe Mickey and Robert Brown of the North Carolina Wildlife Commission, and Gary Swihart of the U.S. Fish and Wildlife Service. The names used are from Robins, et al., *A List of Common and Scientific Names of Fishes from the United States and Canada,* 11th ed. (Bethesda, Md.: American Fisheries Society Special Publication No. 12, 1980).

Species	Otter Cr.– James R.	Rocky Knob	Cone-Price	Linville Falls	Crabtree Meadows
Rainbow trout (*Salmo gairdneri*)	X	X	X	X	
Brown trout (*S. trutta*)		X	X	X	
Brook trout (*Salvelinus fontinalis*)	X	X	X	X	X
Stoneroller (*Campostoma anomalum*)	X		X	X	
Rosyside dace (*Clinostomus funduloides*)	X	X	X	X	
Carp (*Cyprinus carpio*)	X				
Cutlips minnow (*Exoglossum maxillingua*)		X			
Hornyhead chub (*Nocomis biguttatus*)	X	X			
Bluehead chub (*N. leptocephalus*)	X		X		
River chub (*N. micropogon*)		X	X		
Golden shiner (*Notemigonus crysoleucas*)	X		X		
Crescent shiner (*Notropis cerasinus*)		X			
Greenhead shiner (*N. chlorocephalus*)				X	
Warpaint shiner (*N. coccogenis*)				X	
Fieryblack shiner (*N. pyrrhomelas*)				?	
Redfin shiner (*N. umbratilis*)	X				
Mountain redbelly dace (*Phoxinus oreas*)	X				

Species	Otter Cr.-James R.	Rocky Knob	Cone-Price	Linville Falls	Crabtree Meadows
Blacknose dace (*Rhinichthys atratulus*)	X	X	X	X	
Longnose dace (*R. cataractae*)				X	
Creek chub (*Semotilus atromaculatus*)		X	X	?	
Fall fish (*S. corporalis*)		X			
White sucker (*Catostomus commersoni*)	X	X	X	X	
Northern hog sucker (*Hypentelium nigricans*)			X	X	
Silver redhorse (*Moxostoma anisurum*)			X		
Torrent sucker (*M. rhothoecum*)	X	X			
Striped jumprock (*M. rupiscartes*)				?	
Yellow bullhead (*Ictalurus natalis*)	X				
Brown bullhead (*I. nebulosus*)	X				
Margined madtom (*Noturus insignis*)	X			?	
Redbreast sunfish (*Lepomis auritis*)				?	
Warmouth (*L. gulosus*)	X				
Bluegill (*L. macrochirus*)	X		X		
Longear sunfish (*L. megalotis*)	X				
Smallmouth bass (*Micropterus dolomieui*)	X			?	
Largemouth bass (*M. salmoides*)	X		X		
Black crappie (*Pomoxis nigromaculatus*)	X				
Fantail darter (*Etheostoma flabellare*)		X		X	
Longfin darter (*E. longimanum*)	X				
Banded darter (*E. zonale*)	X				
Banded sculpin (*Cottus carolinae*)			X		

Amphibians

Much of the information for this list was supplied by Dr. R. Wayne Van Devender of Appalachian State University, William Palmer of the North Carolina State Museum of Natural History, Costello M. Craig, W.H. Martin, and Tom Haggerty. Other information is from National Park Service records and personnel. Nomenclature follows Collins, et al., *Standard Common and Current Scientific Names for North American Amphibians and Reptiles*, 2nd ed. (n.p., Society for the Study of Amphibians and Reptiles, 1982).

Appendix

Species	Otter Cr.-James R.	Peaks of Otter	Cone-Price	Linville Falls
Hellbender (*Cryptobranchus alleganiensis*)			X	
Spotted salamander (*Ambystoma maculatum*)	X		X	
Eastern newt (*Notophthalmus viridescens*)	E	X	X	X
Northern dusky salamander (*Desmognathus fuscus*)	X	X	X	X
Seal salamander (*D. monticola*)	X	X	X	X
Blackbelly salamander (*D. quadramaculatus*)			X	X
Mountain dusky salamander (*D. ochrophaeus*)			X	X
Pigmy salamander (*D. wrighti*)			X	
Shovelnose salamander (*Leurognathus marmoratus*)			X	X
Redback salamander (*Plethodon cinereus*)	X	X	X	X
Ravine salamander (*P. richmondi*)	X	X	X	
Peaks of Otter salamander (*P. nettingi hubrichti*)		X		
Slimy salamander (*P. glutinosus*)	X	X	X	X
Yonahlossee salamander (*P. yonahlossee*)			X	X
Jordan's salamander (*P. jordani*)			X	X
Four-toed salamander (*Hemidactylium scutatum*)			?	
Spring salamander (*Gyrinophilus porphyriticus*)	X	X	X	X
Red salamander (*Pseudotriton ruber*)	X	X	X	X
Two-lined salamander (*Eurycea bislineata*)	X	X	X	X
Longtail salamander (*E. longicauda*)	X	X	?	
Three-lined salamander (*E. guttolineata*)	X		X	X
American toad (*Bufo americanus*)	X	X	X	X
Fowler's toad (*B. woodhousii*)	X	X	?	
Northern cricket frog (*Acris crepitans*)	X	X		
Spring peeper (*Hyla crucifer*)	X	X	X	X
Gray treefrogs (*H. versicolor, H. chrysoscelis*)	X	E	X	X
Upland chorus frog (*Pseudacris triseriata*)	E	X		
Bullfrog (*Rana catesbeiana*)	X	X	X	X
Green frog (*R. clamitans*)	X	X	X	X
Wood frog (*R. sylvatica*)	X	X	X	X
Pickerel frog (*R. palustris*)	X	X	X	X

Reptiles

Information and nomenclature for the reptile list come from the same sources as those credited for amphibians. As is often the case, the information available on the various recreation areas ranges from excellent to spotty. Only areas whose reptile fauna are relatively well known are included here.

Species	Otter Cr.- James R.	Peaks of Otter	Cone- Price	Linville Falls
Snapping turtle (*Chelydra serpentina*)	X	X	X	X
Stinkpot (*Sternotherus odoratus*)	E			
Bog turtle (*Clemmys muhlenbergii*)			X	
Eastern box turtle (*Terrapene carolina*)	X	X	X	X
Eastern painted turtle (*Chrysemys picta*)	E			
Eastern fence lizard (*Sceloporus undulatus*)	X	X	X	X
Five-lined skink (*Eumeces fasciatus*)	X	X	?	X
Broadhead skink (*E. laticeps*)	X	X		
Northern water snake (*Nerodia sipedon*)	X	X	X	X
Queen snake (*Regina septemvittata*)	X	X	X	?
Brown snake (*Storeria dekayi*)	X			
Redbelly snake (*S. occipitomaculata*)			?	
Eastern garter snake (*Thamnophis sirtalis*)	E	X	X	X
Eastern ribbon snake (*T. sauritis*)			X	
Smooth earth snake (*Virginia valeriae*)		X		
Eastern hognose snake (*Heterodon platyrhinos*)	X	?	?	
Ringneck snake (*Diadophis punctatus*)	X	X	X	X
Worm snake (*Carphophis amoenus*)	E	X	X	
Black racer (*Coluber constrictor*)	X	X	X	X
Rough green snake (*Opheodrys aestivus*)	E	X	E	E
Smooth green snake (*O. vernalis*)	X	E		
Corn snake (*Elaphe guttata*)	E	X		
Black rat snake (*E. obsoleta*)	X	X	X	X
Pine snake (*Pituophis melanoleucus*)		?		
Eastern kingsnake (*Lampropeltis getulus*)	X	X		
Eastern milk snake, scarlet kingsnake (*L. triangulum*)	E		X	X
Mole kingsnake (*L. calligaster*)	X			
Copperhead (*Agkistrodon contortrix*)	X	X	X	X
Timber rattlesnake (*Crotalus horridus*)	X	X	X	X

Birds

Included here are two bird checklists, one for the Mount Pisgah area in North Carolina and one for Virginia's Peaks of Otter. Together, the two lists include most of the birds likely to be found along the Blue Ridge Parkway. The Peaks of Otter list was prepared by members of the Roanoke Valley Bird Club. Information for the Mount Pisgah list was generously provided by Dr. Marcus B.

Simpson, Jr., and Michael Tove. Further information for both lists has come from National Park Service personnel.

Because birds are so mobile, whether or not they can be found in any given place depends a lot on the time of year. Therefore, the lists are organized by seasons:

Sp = Spring (March–May);
 S = Summer (June –August);
 F = Fall (September –November);
 W = Winter (December –February).

The relative abundance of the different species is also indicated:

a = abundant (a common species which is very numerous)

c = common (certain to be seen in suitable habitat)

u = uncommon (present, but not certain to be seen)

o = occasional (seen only a few times during a season)

r = rare (previously recorded in the area but not to be expected)

Names follow the *AOU Check-list of North American Birds,* 5th ed. (Washington, D.C.: American Ornithologists' Union, 1957) and its supplements. Scientific nomenclature is omitted here, since the common names are widely known and used, even among ornithologists.

Mount Pisgah

Species	Sp	S	F	W
Turkey vulture	c	c	c	
Black vulture	r	r	r	
Goshawk				r
Sharp-shinned hawk	u	u	u	u
Cooper's hawk	u	u	u	u
Red-tailed hawk	u	u	u	u
Red-shouldered hawk	r		r	
Broad-winged hawk	u	u	c	
Golden eagle	r	r	r	r
Bald eagle		r	r	
Marsh hawk	o		o	
Osprey	o		o	
Peregrine falcon	r		r	
Merlin	r		r	
American kestrel	o		o	
Ruffed grouse	u	u	u	u
Bobwhite	u	u	u	u

Species	Sp	S	F	W
Turkey	o	o	o	o
American woodcock	c	c	c	
Yellow-billed cuckoo	u	u	u	
Black-billed cuckoo	o	o	o	
Screech owl	u	u	u	u
Barred owl	u	u	u	u
Whip-poor-will	r	r	r	
Common nighthawk	u		u	
Chimney swift	c	c	c	
Ruby-throated hummingbird	u	u	u	
Common flicker	c	c	c	c
Pileated woodpecker	u	u	u	u
Red-headed woodpecker	r		r	
Yellow-bellied sapsucker	o	o	o	o
Hairy woodpecker	o	o	o	o
Downy woodpecker	c	c	c	c
Great crested flycatcher	u	u	u	
Eastern phoebe	u	u	u	
Acadian flycatcher	u	u	u	
Willow flycatcher	o		o	
Alder flycatcher	o		o	
Least flycatcher	o		o	
Eastern wood pewee	u	u	u	
Olive-sided flycatcher	r		r	
Rough-winged swallow	u	u	u	
Barn swallow	u	o	u	
Cliff swallow		r		
Purple martin	u		u	
Blue jay	c	c	c	c
Common raven	c	c	c	c
Common crow	c	c	c	c
Black-capped chickadee	r			
Carolina chickadee	c	c	c	u
Tufted titmouse	c	c	c	c
White-breasted nuthatch	u	u	u	u
Red-breasted nuthatch	u	u	u	u
Brown creeper	u	u	u	u
Winter wren	u	u	u	u
Carolina wren	o	o	o	
Gray catbird	a	a	a	
Brown thrasher	u	u	u	
American robin	a	a	a	u

Species	Sp	S	F	W
Wood thrush	c	c	c	
Hermit thrush	o		o	
Swainson's thrush	u		u	
Gray-cheeked thrush	o		o	
Veery	c	c	c	
Eastern bluebird	o	o	o	r
Blue-gray gnatcatcher	u	u	u	
Golden-crowned kinglet	u	u	u	u
Ruby-crowned kinglet	u		u	c
Water pipit	o		o	
Cedar waxwing	c	c	c	u
White-eyed vireo	o		o	
Solitary vireo	u	u	u	
Red-eyed vireo	c	c	c	
Black-and-white warbler	u	u	u	
Worm-eating warbler	o	o	o	
Golden-winged warbler	o	o	o	
Blue-winged warbler	o		o	
Tennessee warbler	u		u	
Northern parula	u	o	u	
Magnolia warbler	u		u	
Cape May warbler	u		u	
Black-throated blue warbler	u	u	u	
Yellow-rumped warbler	o		o	o
Black-throated green warbler	c	c	c	
Blackburnian warbler	u	u	u	
Chestnut-sided warbler	a	a	a	
Bay-breasted warbler	o		o	
Blackpoll warbler	o		o	
Pine warbler	r	r	r	
Ovenbird	u	u	u	
Louisiana waterthrush	o	o	o	
Common yellowthroat	u	u	u	
Yellow-breasted chat	r	r	r	
Hooded warbler	u	u	u	
Canada warbler	u	u	u	
American redstart	u	o	u	
Bobolink	o		o	
Eastern meadowlark	u		u	
Red-winged blackbird	u		u	
Common grackle	u	u	u	
Brown-headed cowbird	u	u	u	

Species	Sp	S	F	W
Scarlet tanager	u	u	o	
Cardinal	u	u	u	u
Rose-breasted grosbeak	c	c	c	
Indigo bunting	c	c	c	
Purple finch	u		u	u
Pine siskin	o		o	o
American goldfinch	c	c	c	c
Red crossbill	o		o	o
Rufous-sided towhee	c	c	c	u
Vesper sparrow	o		o	u
Dark-eyed junco	a	a	a	a
Chipping sparrow	u	u	u	
Field sparrow	u	u	u	
White-throated sparrow	c		c	c
Fox sparrow	u		u	o
Song sparrow	c	c	c	u

Peaks of Otter

Species	Sp	S	F	W
Common loon	r		r	
Horned grebe			r	
Pied-billed grebe	u		u	
Great blue heron	o	o	o	o
Green heron	o	o	o	
American bittern	r		r	
Whistling swan			r	
Canada goose			r	r
Mallard	o		o	o
Northern shoveler	r		r	
Wood duck	o	o	o	r
Ring-necked duck	r		r	r
Lesser scaup	r		r	r
Bufflehead	o		o	r
Ruddy duck	r		r	
Turkey vulture	c	c	c	c
Black vulture	u	u	u	u
Goshawk			r	r
Sharp-shinned hawk	r	r	c	u
Cooper's hawk	r	r	o	u
Red-tailed hawk	c	c	c	c

Appendix

Species	Sp	S	F	W
Red-shouldered hawk	r		o	r
Broad-winged hawk	u	u	c	
Golden eagle	r		r	
Bald eagle	r		r	
Marsh hawk	r		o	
Osprey	u		u	
Peregrine falcon			r	
American kestrel	o		u	
Ruffed grouse	u	u	u	u
Bobwhite	u	u	u	u
Turkey	u	u	u	u
Virginia rail	r			
Sora	r			
American coot	o		r	o
Killdeer	r	r	r	r
Greater yellowlegs	r		r	
Solitary sandpiper	r		r	
Spotted sandpiper	o		r	
American woodcock	o	o	o	r
Common snipe	r		o	
Least sandpiper	r		r	
Herring gull	r		r	r
Ring-billed gull	r		r	r
Black tern	r		r	
Rock dove	r			
Mourning dove	c	c	u	o
Yellow-billed cuckoo	u	u	u	
Black-billed cuckoo	o	o		
Screech owl	u	u	u	u
Great horned owl	o	o	o	o
Barred owl	u	u	u	u
Chuck-will's-widow	r	r		
Whip-poor-will	o	o		
Common nighthawk			o	
Chimney swift	u	c	u	
Ruby-throated hummingbird	c	u	c	
Belted kingfisher	u	u	u	o
Common flicker	c	c	c	c
Pileated woodpecker	u	u	u	u
Red-bellied woodpecker	c	u	u	c
Red-headed woodpecker			r	
Yellow-bellied sapsucker	o		o	u

Species	Sp	S	F	W
Hairy woodpecker	u	u	u	u
Downy woodpecker	c	c	c	c
Eastern kingbird	u	u	u	
Great crested flycatcher	u	c	u	
Eastern phoebe	c	c	u	c
Yellow-bellied flycatcher	r			
Acadian flycatcher	c	c	c	
Willow flycatcher	r	r		
Least flycatcher		r		
Eastern wood pewee	c	c	c	
Olive-sided flycatcher	r			
Tree swallow	u		o	
Rough-winged swallow	u	u	u	
Barn swallow	a	a	c	
Blue jay	c	a	c	c
Common raven	u	u	u	u
Common crow	a	a	a	a
Fish crow	r		r	
Black-capped chickadee	r		r	r
Carolina chickadee	a	c	c	c
Tufted titmouse	c	c	c	c
White-breasted nuthatch	c	c	c	c
Red-breasted nuthatch	o		o	o
Brown creeper	u		u	u
House wren	o	o	o	
Winter wren	o	r	o	u
Bewick's wren	r	r	r	
Carolina wren	c	c	c	c
Mockingbird	r	o	r	r
Gray catbird	a	a	a	
Brown thrasher	c	c	c	
American robin	u	u	u	u
Wood thrush	c	c	c	
Hermit thrush	o		o	o
Swainson's thrush	u		u	
Gray-cheeked thrush	r		r	
Veery	c	c	u	
Eastern bluebird	c	c	c	u
Blue-gray gnatcatcher	c	c	u	
Golden-crowned kinglet	o		o	u
Ruby-crowned kinglet	o		o	c
Water pipit	r			

Species	Sp	S	F	W
Cedar waxwing	u	u	u	u
Loggerhead shrike	r	r	r	r
Starling	u	u	u	u
White-eyed vireo	u	o	u	
Yellow-throated vireo	u	u	u	
Solitary vireo	u	u	u	
Red-eyed vireo	a	a	c	
Philadelphia vireo			r	
Warbling vireo	r	r	r	
Black-and-white warbler	c	c	u	
Prothonotary warbler	o	o		
Worm-eating warbler	u	u	u	
Golden-winged warbler	o	o	o	
Blue-winged warbler	o	o	o	
Brewster's warbler (hybrid)	r	r		
Tennessee warbler	r		o	
Orange-crowned warbler	r			
Nashville warbler	r		o	
Northern parula	c	c	o	
Yellow warbler	c	c	u	
Magnolia warbler	o		c	
Cape May warbler	u		u	
Black-throated blue warbler	u	u	u	
Yellow-rumped warbler	c		c	o
Black-throated green warbler	u	u	u	
Cerulean warbler	c	c	o	
Blackburnian warbler	u	u	u	
Yellow-throated warbler	o	o		
Chestnut-sided warbler	a	c	c	
Bay-breasted warbler	o		u	
Blackpoll warbler	c		c	
Pine warbler	c	c	u	
Prairie warbler	c	r	o	
Palm warbler	o		o	
Ovenbird	c	c	c	
Northern waterthrush	o		o	
Louisiana waterthrush	c	c	o	
Kentucky warbler	u	u	u	
Mourning warbler	r		r	
Common yellowthroat	a	c	c	
Yellow-breasted chat	c	c	c	
Hooded warbler	c	c	u	

Species	Sp	S	F	W
Wilson's warbler	o		o	
Canada warbler	u	u	u	
American redstart	c	c	c	
House sparrow	o	o	o	o
Bobolink	r			
Eastern meadowlark	o	o	o	
Red-winged blackbird	c	c	u	r
Orchard oriole	o	o	r	
Northern oriole	c	u	u	
Rusty blackbird	r			
Common grackle	c	c	c	u
Brown-headed cowbird	c	c	o	
Scarlet tanager	c	c	u	
Summer tanager	r			
Cardinal	c	c	c	c
Rose-breasted grosbeak	c	c	u	
Blue grosbeak	o	o	o	
Indigo bunting	a	a	c	
Evening grosbeak	o		r	r
Purple finch	o		r	o
Pine siskin	r			r
American goldfinch	c	c	c	u
Red crossbill	r			r
White-winged crossbill				r
Rufous-sided towhee	a	a	a	u
Savannah sparrow			r	r
Grasshopper sparrow	u	u	u	
Vesper sparrow	u			
Dark-eyed junco	c	c	c	c
Chipping sparrow	c	c	c	
Field sparrow	c	c	u	u
White-crowned sparrow	u			
White-throated sparrow	c		u	c
Fox sparrow	o		o	r
Lincoln's sparrow			o	
Swamp sparrow	o		o	
Song sparrow	c	c	c	c

Appendix

Mammals

This list is based on J.L. Chamberlain's unpublished 1969 report for the National Park Service, "Mammals of the Blue Ridge Mountains," and on information from Dr. R. Wayne Van Devender of Appalachian State University, Roger Stone, Tom Haggerty, and National Park Service records and staff. Names follow William H. Burt and Richard P. Grossenheider, *A Field Guide to the Mammals* (Boston: Houghton Mifflin, 1964).

Species	Otter Cr.–James R.	Peaks of Otter	Doughton Park	Cone-Price	Linville Falls
Opossum (*Didelphis marsupialis*)	X	X	X	X	X
Masked shrew (*Sorex cinereus*)	X	E	?	X	E
Smoky shrew (*S. fumeus*)	X	E	E	E	E
Long-tailed shrew (*S. dispar*)	E				?
Pigmy shrew (*Microsorex hoyi*)	?	?	?	?	?
Short-tailed shrew (*Blarina brevicauda*)	X	X	E	X	X
Star-nosed mole (*Condylura cristata*)	E				?
Eastern mole (*Scalopus aquaticus*)	X	X	X	X	X
Hairy-tailed mole (*Parascalops breweri*)				X	X
Little brown bat (*Myotis lucifugus*)	X	X			X
Keen's myotis (*M. keeni*)				?	
Small-footed myotis (*M. subulatus*)				E	
Silver-haired bat (*Lasionycteris noctivagans*)				E	?
Eastern pipistrelle (*Pipistrellus subflavus*)	E			E	
Big brown bat (*Eptesicus fuscus*)	X	E		X	E
Red bat (*Lasiurus borealis*)	X	E	E		?
Evening bat (*Nycticeius humeralis*)	X			E	?
Eastern cottontail (*Sylvilagus floridanus*)	X	X	X	X	X
New England cottontail (*S. transitionalis*)				X	?
Woodchuck (*Marmota monax*)	X	X	X	X	X
Eastern chipmunk (*Tamias striatus*)	X	X	X	X	X
Gray squirrel (*Sciurus carolinensis*)	X	X	X	X	X
Fox squirrel (*S. niger*)	E	X			
Red squirrel (*Tamiasciurus hudsonicus*)		X	X	X	X
Southern flying squirrel (*Glaucomys volans*)	X	X	E	E	E
Beaver (*Castor canadensis*)	X		X		?
Deer mouse (*Peromyscus maniculatus*)				X	X
White-footed mouse (*P. leucopus*)	X	X	X	X	X
Golden mouse (*P. nuttalli*)				E	X

Species	Otter Cr.–James R.	Peaks of Otter	Doughton Park	Cone-Price	Linville Falls
Eastern wood rat (*Neotoma floridana*)	X	X		E	
Hispid cotton rat (*Sigmodon hispidus*)				E	
Bog lemming (*Synaptomys cooperi*)	E	E		E	?
Red-backed mouse (*Cleithrionomys gapperi*)	E	X		E	E
Meadow vole (*Microtus pennsylvanicus*)	X	X	X	X	X
Rock vole (*M. chrotorrhinus*)					?
Pine vole (*M. pinetorum*)	E	X		?	X
Muskrat (*Ondatra zibethica*)	X			X	X
Norway rat (*Rattus norvegicus*)	X			E	
House mouse (*Mus musculus*)	E			E	X
Meadow jumping mouse (*Zapus hudsonicus*)	X	X	E	X	X
Woodland jumping mouse (*Napaeozapus insignis*)	?	?	?	X	?
Gray fox (*Urocyon cinereoargenteus*)	X	X	X	X	X
Red fox (*Vulpes fulva*)	X	E	X	X	X
Black bear (*Ursus americanus*)	X	X	X	X	X
Raccoon (*Procyon lotor*)	X	X	X	X	X
Least weasel (*Mustela rixosa*)	X			X	
Long-tailed weasel (*M. frenata*)	X	E	X	E	E
Mink (*M. vison*)	X	X	X	X	X
River otter (*Lutra canadensis*)	X				
Spotted skunk (*Spilogale putorius*)	?	X	X	X	X
Striped skunk (*Mephitis mephitis*)	X	X	X	X	X
Mountain lion (*Felis concolor*)	?	?			
Bobcat (*Lynx rufus*)	X	X	X	X	X
White-tailed deer (*Odocoileus virginianus*)	X	X	X	X	X

Suggested Reading

General

Brooks, Maurice. *The Appalachians.* Boston: Houghton Mifflin, 1965.
Doolittle, Jerome, and the Editors of Time-Life Books. *The Southern Appalachians.* New York: Time-Life Books, 1975.
Lord, William G. *Blue Ridge Parkway Guide.* Asheville, N.C.: Hexagon, 1976.
McCormick, Jack. *The Life of the Forest.* New York: McGraw-Hill, 1966.
Ogburn, Charlton. *The Southern Appalachians: A Wilderness Quest.* William Morrow, 1975.
Rives, Margaret Rose. *Blue Ridge Parkway: The Story Behind the Scenery.* Las Vegas, Nev.: KC Publications, 1982.

Field Guides

Audubon Society Field Guides. New York: Knopf.
Golden Guides and Golden Field Guides. New York: Golden Press.
Peterson Field Guides. Boston: Houghton Mifflin.

Chapter-by-Chapter Categories

Geology
Cook, Frederick; Larry D. Brown; and Jack E. Oliver. "The Southern Appalachians and the Growth of Continents." *Scientific American,* Oct. 1980.
Dietrich, Richard V. *Geology and Virginia.* Charlottesville: Univ. of Virginia Press, 1970.
King, Philip B.; Robert B. Neuman; and Jarvis B. Hadley. *Geology of the Great Smoky Mountains National Park, Tennessee and North Carolina.* Geological Survey Professional Paper 587. Washington: U.S. Government Printing Office, 1968.

Nonflowering Plants
Hesler, L.R. *Mushrooms of the Great Smokies.* Knoxville: Univ. of Tennessee Press, 1960.
Miller, Orson K., Jr. *Mushrooms of North America.* New York: Dutton, 1978.
Wherry, Edgar T. *The Southern Fern Guide.* Garden City, N.Y.: Doubleday, 1964.

Wildflowers
Gupton, Oscar W., and Fred C. Swope. *Wildflowers of the Shenandoah Valley and Blue Ridge Mountains.* Charlottesville: Univ. of Virginia Press, 1979.

Justice, William S., and C. Ritchie Bell. *Wild Flowers of North Carolina.* Chapel Hill: Univ. of North Carolina Press, 1968.

Stupka, Arthur, and Eastern National Parks and Monuments Association. *Wildflowers in Color.* New York: Harper & Row, 1965.

Trees

Peattie, Donald Culross. *A Natural History of Trees of Eastern and Central North America.* New York: Bonanza Books, 1966.

Wells, B.W. *The Natural Gardens of North Carolina.* Chapel Hill: Univ. of North Carolina Press, 1967.

Fish, Amphibians, and Reptiles

Huheey, James E., and Arthur Stupka. *Amphibians and Reptiles of Great Smoky Mountains National Park.* Knoxville: Univ. of Tennessee Press, 1967.

Martof, Bernard S.; William M. Palmer; Joseph R. Bailey; and Julian R. Harrison III. *Amphibians and Reptiles of the Carolinas and Virginia.* Chapel Hill: Univ. of North Carolina Press, 1980.

Birds

Potter, Eloise F.; James F. Parnell; and Robert P. Teulings. *Birds of the Carolinas.* Chapel Hill: Univ. of North Carolina Press, 1980.

Virginia Society of Ornithology. *Virginia's Birdlife: An Annotated Checklist.* 1979.

Mammals

Handley, Charles O., and Clyde P. Patton. *Wild Mammals of Virginia.* Virginia Commission of Game and Inland Fisheries, 1947.

Linzey, Alicia V., and Donald W. *Mammals of Great Smoky Mountains National Park.* Knoxville: Univ. of Tennessee Press, 1953.

Humans

Jolley, Harley E. *The Blue Ridge Parkway.* Knoxville: Univ. of Tennessee Press, 1969.

Kephart, Horace. *Our Southern Highlanders: A Narrative of Adventure in the Southern Appalachians and a Study of Life among the Mountaineers.* New York: Macmillan, 1929. Reprint. Knoxville: Univ. of Tennessee Press, 1976.

General Index

acorns, 146, 158
adaptations, defined, 147
algae, 29, 30
Alleghany Mountains, 23
Amanitas, 40
amoebae, 89
ants, 43, 58, 92, 145
aphid, balsam woolly, 76–78, 102, 103
Appalachians, central, 7, 9
Appalachians, southern, 7, 22; defined, 9;
    formed, 15–20; plant diversity, 47;
    precipitation, 27; rounded topography,
    21; temperatures, 27
aquamarine, *24, 25*
asbestos, 25
Asheville, N.C., 13, 49, 67, 73, 160, 162
aspect (of slopes) 27; effects on trees, 68
aspen, large-toothed, 81
asters, 57
azalea(s), 48, 54; flame, 51, 54; pinxter-
    flower, 51

bacteria, 43–44; in cooperative relation-
    ships, 44; as decomposers, 44
bald(s), 54, 78–80; causes of, 78–80;
    grassy, 78–80; heath, 78–80; mainte-
    nance of, 79–80
Balsam Mountains, 12, 13, 128
Bartram, John, 47
Bartram, William, 47, 51
bass, 106
basswood, 71, 73
bat(s), 88, 115, 146, 157–158
bear, black, 7, 69, 140, 145–146, 148, 160,
    162, 164
beaver, 146–147
beech, American, 68, 71, 74, 75
bees: role in pollination, 57–60, 103–104;
    burrowing, 60
beetle(s), 87, 98, 99; ground, 90, 104; lo-
    cust leaf miner, 103; as pollinators, 45,
    58; red milkweed, 94; *see also* fireflies
black-eyed Susans, 56

Black Mountains, 12, 74
birch(es), 60; black, *52*; paper, 81; river,
    73; white. *See* paper birch; yellow, 71,
    73, 74, 75
birds, 87, 115, 146, 150; migration, 138–
    139; *see also* specific types
bison. *See* buffalo
blackberries, 56, 61
blackflies, 107
bloodroot, 48
Blowing Rock, N.C., 13
Blue Ridge Mountains: described, 9, 12,
    13; origin of blue color, 67
Blue Ridge physiographic province. *See*
    physiographic provinces
blueberries, 54, 56, 73
bluebirds, eastern, 133
bluejays, 129
bluets, 51
bobcat, 146, 148, 160, 161
boletes, 40
boneset, 56, 92
Boone, Daniel, 141
Boone, N.C., 13
botanists, early, 47–48
bream. *See* sunfish
buckeye, yellow, 71, 74, 75
buffalo, woodland, 141, 159, 162
bugs, milkweed, 94, *96*
building stone, 25
bunting, indigo, 133
Burnsville, N.C., 26
butterfly(ies), 92; great spangled fritillary,
    60; monarch, 92, *93, 94, 95, 96,* 99;
    mourning cloak, 99; painted lady, 94,
    99; pearl crescent, 94; pipevine swallow-
    tail, 92; red admiral, 99; tiger swallow-
    tail, 92; viceroy, 94; *see also* skippers
butterfly weed, 56, 92
Byrd, William, 141

cabbage, skunk, 48
cactus, prickly-pear, 51

Index of Parkway Mileposts

This index will allow you to locate all references made in the text to locations on the Blue Ridge Parkway. Major Parkway recreation areas are shown in boldface type.

Index

A Naturalist's Blue Ridge Parkway was composed on a Compugraphic digital phototypesetter in eleven point Plantin with two points of spacing between the lines. The book was designed by Ed King at Hillside Studio, set into type by Metricomp, Inc., printed offset by Thomson-Shore, Inc., and bound by John H. Dekker & Sons. The paper on which the book is printed carries acid-free characteristics for a projected life of at least three hundred years.

THE UNIVERSITY OF TENNESSEE PRESS : KNOXVILLE